FAITH LESSONS
ON THE death &
resurrection
OF THE messiah

PARTICIPANT'S GUIDE

Also available from Ray Vander Laan

Video and Group Resources

Faith Lessons on the Life and Ministry of the Messiah
Faith Lessons on the Promised Land
Faith Lessons on the Prophets and Kings of Israel

Book and Audiocassette

Echoes of His Presence

FAITH LESSONS
ON THE death &
resurrection
OF THE messiah

PARTICIPANT'S GUIDE

Ray Vander Laan

with

Stephen and Amanda Sorenson

GRAND RAPIDS, MICHIGAN 49530

ZONDERVAN™

Faith Lessons on the Death and Resurrection of the Messiah Participant's Guide
Copyright © 1999 by Ray Vander Laan

Requests for information should be addressed to:

Zondervan, *Grand Rapids, Michigan 49530*

ISBN 0-310-67899-4

Interior design by Sherri Hoffman

Printed in the United States of America

07 08 09 10 11 • 30 29 28 27 26 25 24 23 22 21

contents

Introduction

Because God speaks to us through the Scriptures, studying them is a rewarding experience. The inspired human authors of the Bible, as well as those to whom the words were originally given, were primarily Jews living in the Near East. God's words and actions spoke to them with such power, clarity, and purpose that they wrote them down and carefully preserved them as an authoritative body of literature.

God's use of human servants in revealing Himself resulted in writings that clearly bear the stamp of time and place. The message of the Scriptures is, of course, eternal and unchanging—but the circumstances and conditions of the people of the Bible are unique to their times. Consequently, we most clearly understand God's truth when we know the cultural context within which He spoke and acted and the perception of the people with whom He communicated. This does not mean that God's revelation is unclear if we don't know the cultural context. Rather, by learning how to think and approach life as Abraham, Moses, Ruth, Esther, and Paul did, modern Christians will deepen their appreciation of God's Word. To fully apply the message of the Bible, we must enter the world of the Hebrews and familiarize ourselves with their culture.

That is the purpose of this study. The events and characters of the Bible are presented in their original settings. Although the videos offer the latest archaeological research, this series is not intended to be a definitive cultural and geographical study of the lands of the Bible. No original scientific discoveries are revealed here. The purpose of this study is to help us better understand God's revealed mission for our lives by enabling us to hear and see His words in their original context.

understanding the world of the hebrews

More than 3,800 years ago, God spoke to His servant Abraham: "Go, walk through the length and breadth of the land, for I am giving it to you" (Genesis 13:17). From the outset, God's choice of a Hebrew nomad to begin His plan of salvation (that is still unfolding) was linked to the selection of a specific land where His redemptive work would begin. The nature of God's covenant relationship with His people demanded a place where their faith could be exercised and displayed to all nations so that the world would know of *Yahweh,* the true and faithful God. God showed the same care in preparing a land for His chosen people as He did in preparing a people to live in that land. For us to fully understand God's plan and purpose for His people, we must first understand the nature of the place He selected for them.

By New Testament times, the Jewish people had been removed from the Promised Land by the Babylonians due to Israel's failure to live obediently before God (Jeremiah 25:4–11). The exile lasted seventy years, but its impact upon God's people was astounding. New patterns of worship developed, and scribes and experts in God's law shaped the new commitment to be faithful to Him. The prophets predicted the appearance of a Messiah like King David who would revive the kingdom of the Hebrew people.

But the Promised Land was now home to many other groups of people whose religious practices, moral values, and lifestyles conflicted with those of the Jews. Living as God's witnesses took on added difficulty as Greek, Roman, and Samaritan worldviews mingled with that of the Israelites. The Promised Land was divided between kings and governors, usually under the authority of one foreign empire or another. But the mission of God's people did not change. They were still to live *so that the world would know that their God was the true God.* And the land continued to provide them opportunity to encounter the world that desperately needed to know this reality.

The Promised Land was the arena within which God's people were to serve Him faithfully as the world watched. The land God chose for His people was on the crossroads of the world. A major trade route, the Via Maris, ran through it. God intended for the Israelites to take control of the cities along this route and thereby exert influence on the nations around them. Through their righteous living, the Hebrews were to reveal the one true God, *Yahweh,* to the world. They failed to accomplish this mission, however, because of their unfaithfulness.

Western Christianity tends to spiritualize the concept of the Promised Land as it is presented in the Bible. Instead of seeing it as a crossroads from which to influence the world, modern Christians view it as a distant, heavenly city, a glorious "Canaan" toward which we are traveling as we ignore the world around us. We are focused on the destination, not the journey. We have unconsciously separated our walk with God from our responsibility to the world in which He has placed us. In one sense, our earthly experience is simply preparation for an eternity in the "promised land." Preoccupation with this idea, however, distorts the mission God has set for us.

Living by faith is not a vague, otherworldly experience; rather, it is being faithful to God right now, in the place and time in which He has put us. This truth is emphasized by God's choice of Canaan, a crossroads of the ancient world, as the Promised Land for the Israelites. God wants His people to be in the game, not on the bench. Our mission, as Christians today, is the same one He gave to the Israelites. We are to live obediently *within* the world so that through us *the world may know that our God is the one true God.*

The Assumptions of Biblical Writers

Biblical writers assumed that their readers were familiar with Near Eastern geography. The geography of Canaan shaped the culture of the people living there. Their settlements began near sources of water and food. Climate and raw materials shaped their choice of occupation, dress, weapons, diet, and even artistic expression. As their cities grew, they interacted politically. Trade developed, and trade routes were established.

During New Testament times, the Promised Land was called Palestine or Judea. *Judea* (which means "Jewish") technically referred to the land that had been the nation of Judah. Because of the influence that the people of Judea had over the rest of the land, the land itself was called Judea. The Romans divided the land into several provinces, including Judea, Samaria, and Galilee (the three main divisions during Jesus' time); Gaulanitis, the Decapolis, and Perea (east of the Jordan River); and Idumaea (Edom) and Nabatea (in the south). These further divisions of Israel added to the rich historical and cultural background God prepared for the coming of Jesus and the beginning of His church.

Today the names *Israel* and *Palestine* are often used to designate the land God gave to Abraham. Both terms are politically charged. *Palestine* is used by the Arabs living in the central part of the country, while *Israel* is used by the Jews to indicate the State of Israel. In this study, *Israel* is used in the biblical sense. This choice does not indicate a political statement regarding the current struggle in the Middle East but instead is chosen to best reflect the biblical designation for the land.

Unfortunately, many Christians do not have even a basic geographical knowledge of the region. This series is designed to help solve that problem. We will be studying the people and events of the Bible in their geographical and historical contexts. Once we know the *who*, *what*, and *where* of a Bible story, we will be able to understand the *why*. By deepening our understanding of God's Word, we can strengthen our relationship with God.

The biblical writers also used a language that, like all languages, is bound by culture and time. Therefore, understanding the Scriptures involves more than knowing what the words mean. We need to also understand those words from the perspective of the people who used them.

The people whom God chose as His instruments—the people to whom He revealed Himself—were Hebrews living in the Near East. These people described their world and themselves in concrete terms. Their language was one of pictures, metaphors, and examples rather than ideas, definitions, and abstractions. Whereas we might describe God as omniscient or omnipresent (knowing everything and present everywhere), a Hebrew would have preferred to describe God by saying, "The Lord is my shepherd." Thus, the Bible is filled with concrete images from Hebrew culture: God is our Father, and we are His children; God is the potter, and we are the clay; Jesus is the Lamb killed on Passover; heaven is an oasis in the desert, and hell is the city sewage dump; the Last Judgment will be in the Eastern Gate of the heavenly Jerusalem and will include sheep and goats.

These people had an Eastern mindset rather than a Western mindset. Eastern thought emphasizes the process of learning as much or more than the end result. Whereas Westerners tend to collect information to find the right answer, Hebrew thought stresses the process of discovery as well as the answer. So as you go through this study, use it as an opportunity to deepen your understanding of who God is and to grow in your relationship with Him.

when storms come

questions to think about

1. Each of us faces difficulties—what we could label "storms"—in life. Which "storms" do people today face? Just give one- or two-word answers.

2. What difficulties or "storms" frighten you most deeply? To what underlying spiritual force do you attribute those storms?

3. In what ways do evil forces impact your life? Where do you see Satan's power influencing your life?

video notes

Perceptions of Water

The Disciples' Catch

The Disciples' Terrifying Night

Peter's Courage

video Highlights

On the map of the Sea of Galilee note the location of Capernaum (the departure point for Jesus' disciples) and Bethsaida (their destination). Also note the location of Gennesaret, about seven miles away, where they finally ended up the next morning.

1. In the video, Ray Vander Laan said, "We need to row in the direction we think God wants us to go. But there will be times we'll end up in different places than we expected Him to take us." If you can, briefly describe a time in your life when you did your best to follow Jesus toward a specific goal, but ended up in a very different situation.

2. Why do you think Jesus allowed the disciples to row against the threatening waves for hours without the relief He could have provided? What might we learn from that?

3. A first-century disciple wanted more than anything to be like his rabbi. In light of his desire to be like Jesus, what do you think went through Peter's mind when he stepped out of the boat? When he started to sink and he called out to Jesus for help?

4. Toward the end of the video, the Israeli fisherman demonstrated how to use a fishing net correctly. What does practice have to do with bringing Jesus' love to people?

small Group Bible Discovery

Topic A: A New Calling for Fishermen

1. In fulfillment of the prophecy found in Isaiah 9:1–2, in which region did Jesus focus His preaching ministry? (See Matthew 4:12–17; refer to map on page 17.)

PROFILE OF TWO KINDS OF FISHERMEN	
Fishermen of Galilee	Fishermen of God
Fishermen used different kinds of nets and methods (seine nets, circular cast nets, trammel nets, hook and line, spears) to catch different kinds of fish (Job 18:8; Ecclesiastes 9:12; Isaiah 19:8; Matthew 17:24–27; John 21:6–7).	God wants us to use care, dedication, and skill in "fishing" for people who are not yet Christians (Matthew 13:47; Mark 1:16–18; Luke 5:10).
Fishermen fished in the heat of summer and the cold of winter, and at different times of the day to catch different types of fish (John 21:3–6; Luke 5:5–6).	God wants us to vary our approaches to sharing Jesus in order to reach different types of people and guide them into the kingdom of God.
Sometimes fishermen caught fish, sometimes they didn't (John 21:3–6; Luke 5:5–6).	When we share Christ, people respond to Him at some times, at other times they don't.
Fishermen fished from the shore and from boats.	As "fishers of men," we use different means to "fish" — radio, television, one-to-one evangelism, etc.
Fishermen threw away the bad fish they caught (Matthew 13:48).	One day, God's angels will separate the righteous from the unrighteous and throw the unrighteous into the fiery furnace (Matthew 13:49–50).

2. What did Jesus ask the two brothers to do, and how did they respond? (See Matthew 4:18–20; Mark 1:16–18.)

3. How did the two sons of Zebedee respond to Jesus' call? What does their response reveal about their attitude toward Jesus and their commitment to Him? (See Matthew 4:21–22.)

4. In what ways had the brothers' occupation prepared them to understand and fulfill the mission Jesus had in store for them—that of becoming "fishers of men"? (See Mark 1:16–18; Luke 5:1–11.)

5. How does the commitment shown by Peter, Andrew, James, and John when they heard Jesus' call differ from that of many would-be disciples? (See Matthew 4:20, 22.)

DATA FILE

The Sea of Galilee

- Is more than twelve miles long from north to south and nearly eight miles wide at its widest point. The surface is nearly 700 feet below sea level, and it is more than 150 feet deep in some places.

- Is subject to sudden storms caused by an east wind that brings cool air over the warmer blanket of air that covers the lake. The heavier cold air drops as the warm air rises, which causes great air turbulence and violent storms.

- Is the locale where Jesus lived and conducted most of His ministry. He performed ten of His thirty-three recorded miracles in the region.

- Although called a "sea," is really a freshwater lake, fed primarily by the Jordan River in the north. The Sea of Galilee teems with fish today, just as it did during Jesus' time.

- Is deep blue in color and is surrounded by fertile hills and mountains where several hot mineral springs can be found.

Topic B: The Symbols of the Sea

To the Jewish mind in biblical times, the sea represented evil. So in Scripture the sea was used to symbolize the forces of evil in much the same way that a shepherd, rock, and living water were used to represent God. Let's take a look at the symbolic significance of the sea in Scripture.

1. Describe how the evil of the "sea" is personified in these verses:

   Psalm 74:13–14

   Isaiah 27:1

   Daniel 7:2–7

   Revelation 13:1–2

2. What are some of the similarities between the Abyss and the sea? (See Revelation 11:3–7; 17:8; 20:1–3.)

3. In Matthew 11:20–24, what condemnation did Jesus promise to those people who lived in Capernaum, at the edge of the sea, and had heard His message but did not repent?

4. Read Luke 8:27–33, which records an incident involving Jesus, the forces of evil, and the sea.

    a. When Jesus confronted the demon-possessed man, where did the demons beg Jesus not to send them?

    b. Where did the demons want to go instead?

    c. What happened when Jesus gave the demons permission to go there?

Topic C: God Is the Deliverer and Tamer of the Sea

The people of Jesus' day believed that God alone could rescue them from the evil of the sea.

1. What do we learn about water in Psalm 24:1–2 and Genesis 1:2, 6–10?

2. How did God use water to punish sinful people? (See Genesis 7; Exodus 14:23–28.)

3. When did God use water to save His people? (See Exodus
    14:5–9, 27–30; Psalm 77:19–20; Isaiah 51:10.)

4. Which water-related terms in the following verses are used
    to describe difficulties and despair or the way in which
    God brought miraculous deliverance when people called
    on Him for help?
    Psalm 30:1

    Psalm 69:1–3

    Psalm 65:5–7

    Psalm 77:16–20

    Isaiah 51:10

    Jonah 2:1–6

Topic D: The Value of Seeking God in a Solitary Place

In this video, we learned that Jesus went to a solitary place to be with
His Father while His disciples set out to cross the Sea of Galilee. He
often sought a solitary place to pray—sometimes alone, sometimes
with His disciples. Although He was divine, Jesus was also human, so
He experienced the same things we experience. He became weary

physically and emotionally and needed the strength and encouragement of His heavenly Father.

1. Why was it vitally important for Jesus to spend time alone
    with His Father as he faced the following situations?

    Matthew 14:6–13

    Matthew 14:14–23

    Mark 1:23–25, 29–38

    Luke 6:12

    Luke 22:39–46

2. Why did Jesus go to such "lonely places"? (See Mark 1:40–
    45.)

3. After Jesus spent time alone with His Father, what did He
    usually do? (See Matthew 14:13–14, 19–21, 34–36; Mark
    1:35–42.)

4. If you spent more time alone with God in a "lonely place,"
    how might your life be different?

faith Lesson

Time for Reflection

The following Scripture passage describes the storm the disciples faced on the Sea of Galilee. Read this passage silently and consider how you respond to the storms in your life.

> Immediately Jesus made his disciples get into the boat and go on ahead of him to Bethsaida, while he dismissed the crowd. After leaving them, he went up on a mountainside to pray. When evening came, the boat was in the middle of the lake, and he was alone on land. He saw the disciples straining at the oars, because the wind was against them. About the fourth watch of the night he went out to them, walking on the lake. He was about to pass by them, but when they saw him walking on the lake, they thought he was a ghost. They cried out, because they all saw him and were terrified. Immediately he spoke to them and said, "Take courage! It is I. Don't be afraid."

> MARK 6:45–50

> "Lord, if it's you," Peter replied, "tell me to come to you on the water." "Come," he said. Then Peter got down out of the boat, walked on the water and came toward Jesus. But when he saw the wind, he was afraid and, beginning to sink, cried out, "Lord, save me!" Immediately Jesus reached out his hand and caught him. "You of little faith," he said, "why did you doubt?" And when they climbed into the boat, the wind died down. Then those who were in the boat worshiped him, saying, "Truly you are the Son of God." When they had crossed over, they landed at Gennesaret.

> MATTHEW 14:28–34

1. Given the mindset of their culture—the evil that the storm-swept sea represented to them—can you imagine how terrified the disciples must have been when they first saw Jesus? Which situations and circumstances in your life are frightening to you? How do you respond when you come face-to-face with those fears?

2. As you face difficult "storms" in your life that threaten to overwhelm you, which truths about God's knowledge, power, and care for you that we explored in this lesson encourage you to persevere?

3. The disciples had already seen Jesus' power demonstrated in many ways, yet when Jesus calmed the sea, they exclaimed, "Truly you are the Son of God" (Matthew 14:33). What have you seen God do that causes you to marvel and worship Him?

DATA FILE

Galilean Boat

Remains of a first-century boat of the type the disciples would have used have been found in the mud of the Sea of Galilee. Imagine what it would have been like to be one of the disciples on that stormy night!

- The wooden boat is twenty-six feet long and seven-and-one-half feet wide.
- It would have had a crew of five: four members would have rowed at the two pairs of oars, the fifth would have steered. It also carried a small sail.
- The boat could have held several people in addition to the crew.
- A cushion could be placed on the small deck at either end of the boat so a person could sleep.
- The sides of the boat were low to make it easier to cast nets over the side and draw them in. Waves did not have to be high to threaten the boat!

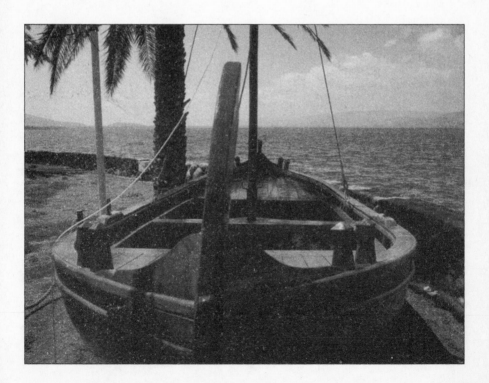

Action Points

Take a moment to review the key points you explored today. Then write down the action step (or steps) that you will commit to this week as a result of what you have discovered.

1. *God's power is greater than any evil, greater than any of the storms of life that we face.* Jesus demonstrated this truth to His disciples by controlling the forces of nature and calming the stormy Sea of Galilee—which represented the power of evil.

   The storm that most frightens me right now is _____
   _____
   _____ .

   Each day this week, I will talk to God about this storm. I will praise Him for the power He has over every evil against which I struggle. I will ask Him to help me face the storm and thank Him that I can count on His help.

2. *Even though God is always with us and watching us, He sometimes allows us to struggle—just as He allowed the disciples to struggle against the waves.* God uses storms in our lives as part of His plan. He uses them to teach us:
   - to depend on Him.
   - to have faith in His plan for our lives.
   - to call out to Him for help.
   - to remind us that we need Him and can't handle everything on our own.
   - to commit ourselves to practice and persevere—to do whatever it takes to accomplish that which He has given us to do.

   List several storms of life that you have faced (or are facing). Next to each write out the lesson God has taught you.

My Storms	God's Lessons

3. *God wants us to follow Him courageously, to step out in faith and do His will.* Just as Peter stepped out of the boat in faith, we have the opportunity to courageously pursue God and do what He calls us to do. Doing so may take us into entirely new directions than what we expect—in relationships, career, evangelism, etc.—just as it took the disciples to Gennesaret instead of Bethsaida.

   Peter took a courageous step of faith—right into the raging waves—when he approached Jesus.

   Which courageous step is God calling you to take?

   What do you fear as you consider where that step will take you?

   What does it mean to you that God is more powerful than any evil you may face?

   From what do you need to ask Him to save you?

piercing the darkness

questions to think about

1. Why do you think many Christians keep company with other Christians instead of going to where non-Christians are and sharing Christ with them?

2. In which segments of our culture do you think Satan and his evil influence is particularly active?

3. What one place seems so evil to you that you would never want to go to it?

4. What would go through your mind if you were walking next to Jesus one day and He announced: "Today, we're going to *that* place"?

video notes

The Decapolis

Jesus' Feeding of the 5,000 and 4,000

The Trip "Across the Sea"

The Demon-Possessed Man

Jesus' Call to Confront Evil

video Highlights

Look at the map of the land of Israel and the Decapolis. Note the area of the Decapolis in relationship to Capernaum and the Sea of Galilee. Note the location of Beth Shan, Susita, Gadara, Gerasa (Jerash)—several key cities of the Decapolis district.

1. From whom, according to one rabbinic tradition, did the people of the Decapolis descend?

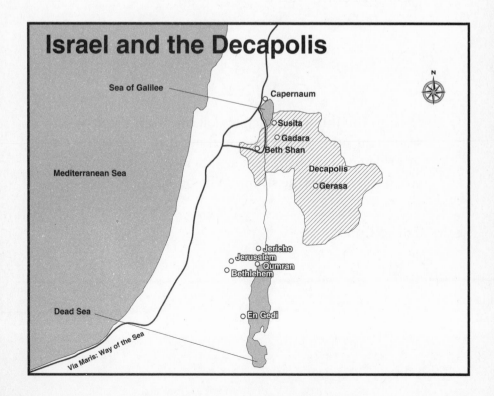

2. What did the Jews think about the Decapolis district? Why?

3. Why did the disciples think of the Decapolis as "the other side"?

4. Why did Jesus sail to the Decapolis district? What can we learn from His desire to take His disciples into the most pagan area of His world?

5. How do you think the disciples felt about going across the sea to "the other side"? Do you think they were surprised that a demon-possessed man met them almost immediately after Jesus calmed the storm? Why or why not?

small group Bible Discovery

Topic A: The Power of One

1. What kind of a response did Jesus and His disciples receive when they returned to "the other side" a while after Jesus healed the demon-possessed man? (See Mark 7:31–36; Matthew 15:30.)

2. How had the people in the entire Decapolis district heard about Jesus? (See Luke 8:38–39; Mark 5:18–20.)

3. What, according to this biblical story, is the key to evangelism?

4. What seems unusual or surprising to you about the way in which God used this one man to establish a strong Christian community in a pagan culture?

5. What can we learn from the spiritual impact of one formerly demon-possessed man who knew no theology yet became an effective missionary in this most pagan area of first-century Israel?

Topic B: Jesus' Commitment to Confronting Evil

1. Immediately after Jesus defeated the storm—the power of evil manifested by the sea—whom did He meet? Explain the possible link between these two events. (See Mark 5:1–13; Luke 8:26–33.)

2. In Luke 8:30–33, the sea into which the demonized pigs ran is referred to as what region?

    a. What does the word *Abyss* symbolize in the book of Revelation? (See Revelation 9:1–3, 11; 11:7; 17:8; 20:1–4.)

    b. What, then, is the significance of the pigs rushing into the sea and drowning?

3. Jesus had demonstrated His power over demons many times. Two such accounts are recorded in Mark 1:21–28 and Mark 9:14–29. Please read these accounts and answer the following questions.

    a. Did the demons recognize who Jesus was? How did they respond to Him?

    b. How did Jesus confront the demons? What was the result?

    c. What was the people's response?

    d. What difficulty had the disciples faced in casting out the demon that possessed the boy? What was the solution?

4. What can we learn from Jesus' confrontation with evil that applies to our lives today? (See Matthew 4:23–25.)

Topic C: A Man Who Had Deep Needs

1. Describe the condition of the demon-possessed man. In what way(s) might he have posed a threat to Jesus and His disciples? (See Mark 5:1–5.)

2. How did the man react to Jesus? Why? (See Mark 5:6–8; Luke 8:28.)

DATA FILE

The History of the Decapolis

Alexander the Great established a Greek presence in the Decapolis in 330 B.C. The Roman general Pompey organized that league of city-states and assumed control of the area in 64–63 B.C. in order to control the trade route from Arabia to Damascus and to protect the eastern frontier. Although the Decapolis comprised more than ten city-states during much of its history, it retained the original name. During New Testament times, the pagan cities in the Decapolis—located to the south and east of the Sea of Galilee—remained a league of free city-states under the umbrella of Roman authority.

The Glory of the Decapolis

Today the ruins of the Decapolis district (derived from the Greek word *Decapolis* that meant "ten cities") still provide evidence of its Greek splendor and seductive, Hellenistic allure:

- A fifteen-mile-long aqueduct brought water to Susita, a city built on a thirty-five-acre plateau. One of the modern Hellenistic cities of the Decapolis, Susita boasted pagan temples, magnificent examples of Greek architecture, paved streets, and fountains.
- In other cities, temples honored local gods and glorified the excesses of pleasure.
- Located about five miles from the Sea of Galilee, the beautiful bath complex at Hammat Gader used hot mineral springs from the nearby Gilead Mountains. At least eight pools—including one more than 100 feet long that featured thirty-two marble fountains—soothed bathers, who no doubt came to the region to find healing in the warm baths and to worship their gods of healing.
- Colonnaded streets, running water, and marble fountains were common in the cities of the Decapolis, as were buildings such as theaters, stadiums, and temples that represented Greek ideals.

The Culture of the Decapolis

The cities of the Decapolis were fully immersed in Greek culture. Hellenism—the humanistic religion of the Greeks—glorified sexuality, the human form, and the excesses of pleasure, violence, and wealth. It preached that truth could be known only through the human mind and that pleasure was a crucial goal in life. Festivals that celebrated pagan holidays and theaters that portrayed erotic themes were a part of daily life in the Decapolis.

Although the religious Jews of Jesus' day opposed the values and practices of Hellenism, the Greek educational system of the region had instilled Greek ideas into generations of young Jewish people. Young Jews read Greek mythology and philosophy and learned to draw and sculpt the forms of Greek gods. The Pharisees, who were devoted to keeping God's people faithful to Torah, constantly admonished young Jews who were intrigued by Greek culture.

Hope for the Decapolis

Jesus deliberately brought the gospel to the people in this region because they needed the "therapy" that He alone could provide. The pagan gods and ideals of Hellenism provided only a false hope.

- After Jesus met a demon-possessed man and drove out his demons, the man told the inhabitants of a nearby city (probably Susita) what had happened to him (Mark 5:1–20). Perhaps as a result of seeing the demon-possessed man healed, a number of people became Christians, making the city a center of early Christianity. Remains of at least five large churches have been found in Susita.
- When people found no cure in the baths at Hammat Gader, some of them turned to Jesus, whose healing powers were known in the Decapolis (Mark 7:31–37). Even though the culture of the Decapolis was sophisticated and offered "healing" for some people, the people needed Jesus' healing power most of all.

3. What was the name of the demons? (See Mark 5:9.)

DATA FILE

Who is Beelzebub?

- Baal-Zebul was the god of the Philistines and means "Exalted Baal" or "Prince Baal."
- The Hebrew name *Baal-Zebub* is a parody of Baal-Zebul and means "Lord of the Flies" (2 Kings 1:2–4).
- In the Greek language of the New Testament, the name becomes *Beelzebub*. Jesus used the name *Beelzebub* for Satan, the prince of demons. (See Matthew 10:25; 12:24–27; Mark 3:22; Luke 11:14–26.) This usage seems to indicate that Old Testament Baal worship was satanic—a tool Satan used to draw the Israelite people away from God.

What Is His Goal?

- First and foremost, Satan is the enemy of God's plan of salvation.
- He has devoted himself to destroying God's plan of salvation since the temptation of Adam and Eve in the Garden of Eden (Genesis 3).
- He tried to use Herod to kill baby Jesus (Matthew 2:13–18).
- He tempted Jesus at the beginning of His ministry, hoping that Jesus would compromise His mission (Matthew 4:1–11).

How Did Jesus Confront Him?

Jesus confronted Satan directly while He was on earth and had numerous confrontations with Satan's demons as well:

- He cast the demon out of the man in the synagogue (Mark 1:23–28).
- He cast a "legion" of demons out of the man of the tombs (Mark 5:1–20).
- He cast a demon out of a boy who couldn't speak and had seizures (Mark 9:14–29).
- He cast many demons out of people after He healed Peter's mother-in-law (Matthew 8:16).

4. After Jesus sent the demons away, how did the man change? (See Luke 8:34–35.)

5. Why do you think the local people reacted as they did to the healing of this man? (See Luke 8:35–37.)

6. How was Jesus received during His second visit? What accounted for the difference? (See Mark 5:18–20; 7:31–37; Matthew 15:29–31.)

Topic D: Old Testament Heroes Who Confronted Evil*

1. *Elijah* (See 1 Kings 18:16–40.)

   a. What was the evil Elijah confronted? What did he say to King Ahab and the Israelites? (See 1 Kings 18:16–21.)

   b. What "test" did Elijah propose? (See 1 Kings 18:22–25.)

---

*Note: Other examples of Old Testament people who confronted evil include: Deborah (Judges 4), Esther (Esther 3:8–11; 4; 5:1–8; 7:1–10), and Josiah (2 Chronicles 34:1–11, 29–33).

c. What was the result? (See 1 Kings 18:26–40.)

2. *David* (See 1 Samuel 17.)

a. Who did Satan use to defy Israel and their God? (See 1 Samuel 17:4–10.)

b. Who battled the giant? Why? By whose power was the giant killed? (See 1 Samuel 17:32–37, 45–50.)

3. *Phinehas* (See Numbers 25:1–13.)

a. What were the Israelites doing that was evil in the sight of God? (See Numbers 25:1–3.)

b. What strong measures did God order to confront this evil? (See Numbers 25:4–5.)

c. What did Phinehas do? What was the result? (See Numbers 25:6–9.)

ƒaith Lesson

Time for Reflection

The following passage of Scripture portrays Jesus as He pierced the darkness of evil in His world. Read this passage silently and take the next few minutes to consider your response to the evil that surrounds you.

A furious squall came up, and the waves broke over the boat, so that it was nearly swamped. Jesus was in the stern, sleeping on a cushion. The disciples woke him and said to him, "Teacher, don't you care if we drown?" He got up, rebuked the wind and said to the waves, "Quiet! Be still!" Then the wind died down and it was completely calm. He said to his disciples, "Why are you so afraid? Do you still have no faith?" They were terrified and asked each other, "Who is this? Even the wind and the waves obey him!" They went across the lake to the region of the Gerasenes. When Jesus got out of the boat, a man with an evil spirit came from the tombs to meet him. . . . When he saw Jesus from a distance, he ran and fell on his knees in front of him. He shouted at the top of his voice, "What do you want with me, Jesus, Son of the Most High God? Swear to God that you won't torture me!" For Jesus had said to him, "Come out of this man, you evil spirit!" Then Jesus asked him, "What is your name?" "My name is Legion," he replied, "for we are many." And he begged Jesus again and again not to send them out of the area. A large herd of pigs was feeding on the nearby hillside. The demons begged Jesus, "Send us among the pigs; allow us to go into them." He gave them permission, and the evil spirits came out and went into the pigs. The herd, about two thousand in number, rushed down the steep bank into the lake and were drowned. Those tending the pigs ran off and reported this in the town and countryside, and the people went out to see what had happened. When they came to Jesus, they saw the man who had been possessed by the legion of demons, sitting there, dressed and in his right mind; and they were afraid. . . . As Jesus was getting into the boat, the man who had been demon-possessed begged to go with him. Jesus did not let him, but said, "Go home to your family and tell them how much the Lord has done for you, and how he has had mercy on you." So the man went away and began to tell in the Decapolis how much Jesus had done for him. And all the people were amazed.

MARK 4:37–5:2; 5:6–15, 18–20

1. Life is a spiritual battleground between good and evil—God and Satan. Are you active in the battle, or are you "on the sidelines"?

2. When you come face-to-face with evil, are you, like the disciples, afraid that Jesus will allow you to perish? What message from this session can help strengthen your faith and bolster your courage when evil threatens?

3. What does this session teach about the impact that one person can have if he or she has a grateful heart and a desire to serve God?

4. What keeps you from sharing what Jesus has done for you with the people you see every day? With whom might God want you to share what He has done for you?

5. What might be the impact on your culture if you were to confront evil whenever you encounter it? If you do not challenge evil?

Action Points

Take a moment to review the key points you explored today. Then write down the action step (or steps) that you will commit to this week as a result of what you have discovered.

1. *Jesus—the light of the world (John 8:12) deliberately and boldly pierced the spiritual darkness of pagan Decapolis.* With great authority, He appropriated God's power to confront and defeat the devil on his own turf—on the sea and among the pagan people of the Decapolis. As a result, many people wanted Him to leave, but one man was delivered into a new life.

Sometimes it is easy to ignore rampant evil around us and hide in our "safe" communities and churches. At other times, it's easy to compromise with sin. God, however, calls His people to boldly confront the power of evil wherever it is. He calls us to be His people in a culture that doesn't hold His values. He calls us to respond compassionately and appropriately to both personal evil—such as immorality, injustice, and hatred—and natural evil—such as death and disease. When we do that, we can expect people to resist and resent us—and the message of Christ that we bring.

Are you willing to step out of your secure environment, to interact with people who hold vastly different values, or to pierce the darkness of a place with which you are unfamiliar and uncomfortable? Armed with the power and name of Jesus, will you allow God to use you to confront immorality, hatred, injustice, and other evils? If so, what might He be calling you to do?

2. *The ministry of one person is powerful!* After healing the demon-possessed man, Jesus told him to go home and tell people what God had done for him. As a result of the man's obedience, many people were drawn to Christ, and a strong Christian community developed in the Decapolis.

In fact, that area of the Decapolis became a cornerstone of the early Christian church. Representatives from the Decapolis served on the early church councils that helped define the important creeds of Christianity and establish the canon, the books that are in the Bible today!

God asks us to tell other people what He has done for us. When we do that, He can work miracles. His light can pierce the darkest evil. Just as that one man made an eternal difference in his pagan community, you can make an eternal difference in your community. What has Jesus done for you that you can share with others? What is your commitment to testify of what God has done for you?

gates of Hades (Hell)

questions to think about

1. As you consider the Christian church today, would you say that it is on the offensive against evil, or has it taken a defensive position? Explain your answer and give examples to illustrate it.

2. Many people through the centuries have boldly attacked the forces of evil for the sake of the gospel. Name some biblical characters or more contemporary people who have made an impact for God by confronting evil in their worlds. Also identify the evil they confronted.

3. Think about what represents evil in your world. What are some of the ways Christians could boldly stand against those evils in the name and power of Jesus—in their neighborhoods, workplaces, or schools?

video notes

The Evil of Caesarea Philippi

Jesus' Message to His Disciples

The Mission of the Church

video нighlights

Look at the map of the region around the Sea of Galilee and note how far Caesarea Philippi was from Capernaum and the Sea of Galilee. Note also Mount Hermon, the beginnings of the Jordan River, and the city of Dan.

1. What do you think the disciples thought as they traveled with Jesus to Caesarea Philippi?

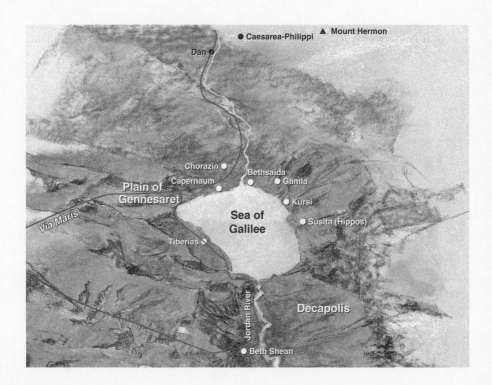

2. Which part of the video made the greatest impact on you? Why?

3. How does the perspective that the church is to take the offensive rather than the defensive against the "gates of hell" affect your view of ministry? How do you think it affected the disciples' view?

small Group Bible Discovery

Topic A: Jesus as Messiah

1. Which roles, according to the prophet Zechariah, would the Messiah fulfill? (See Deuteronomy 18:18; Zechariah 6:13.)

2. After Jesus asked His disciples who people said He was, why do you think He asked His disciples who they thought He was? (See Matthew 16:15; Mark 8:29.)

3. What was the significance of Peter's response to Jesus' second question? (See Matthew 16:16; Mark 8:29.)

4. After Peter made his profession, what did Jesus do? Why do you think He picked this moment to begin explaining this? (See Matthew 16:21–26.)

5. What kind of life did Isaiah the prophet predict that Jesus would have? (See Isaiah 53:1–12.)

6. In light of Isaiah 53:1–12, why do you think it was so difficult for the people of Jesus' day, including the disciples, to understand what He—the Messiah—was called to do?

DATA FILE

Jesus Christ the Messiah

As English-speaking Christians, we refer to our Savior as *Jesus Christ* and *Messiah*. There is great richness of meaning behind these three words.

Jesus is the English form of the name found in Greek versions of the New Testament. The Hebrew name translated *Jesus* was *Yeshua*, a shortened version of the word *Y'hoshua*, which means "Yahweh saves," and in English is translated *Joshua*.

Christ is the English translation of the Greek word *Christos*, which means *Messiah*. Therefore the words *Messiah* and *Christ* are the same, although *Messiah* better reflects the Jewish setting of Jesus' ministry.

Messiah means "anointed" and is rooted in the Old Testament. It refers to the pouring (anointing) of oil on people who were marked by God as uniquely qualified for a task or office. This anointing was a symbol of the authority a person received from God. (That's why Jesus' baptism is so significant—Matthew 3:13–17.) Every anointed person (e.g., prophet, priest, and king) was, in the sense of having been anointed, *a* messiah. The prophets predicted that one day God would send His deliverer— "the ultimate Messiah"—who would combine the roles of prophet, priest, and king. However, the people of Jesus' day emphasized the kingly role of Messiah, whom they believed would deliver them from the political oppression of Rome.

Topic B: The Meanings of the Rock

1. On what did Jesus promise to build His church? (See Matthew 16:18.)

2. There are two major viewpoints concerning what Jesus meant by the "rock" upon which He would build His church. What does the Bible say about:

   a. Peter—representing all the disciples—being the "rock"? (See Ephesians 2:20–21.)

   b. Peter's profession—that Jesus is the Christ, the Son of the living God—being the "rock"? (See 1 Corinthians 3:10–15; Acts 4:10–11.)

3. What is the significance of the description "*this* rock" in Matthew 16:18?

4. The imagery of the "rock" was not new to the disciples.

   a. On which "rock" was the nation of Israel built? (See Isaiah 51:1–2.)

b. Read Psalm 18:2–3. Who is the "rock" whom David
    praised? How does David describe that "rock"?

Topic C: The Gates of Hades (Hell)

Hades—originally the Greek god of the underworld—is the name-
sake for the place where departed spirits live and was frequently used
in the Bible as a synonym for hell or the grave (Psalm 9:17; 55:15;
116:3). As Jesus used it in Matthew 16:18, *Hades* seems to refer to the
powers of evil that resisted Jesus, including Satan's ultimate weapon—
physical death.

1. What did Jesus say His church would have to confront?
    (See Matthew 16:18.)

    a. What did Jesus say would be the outcome?

    b. How can we be assured of this outcome? (See 1 John
        3:7–8; 4:2–4.)

2. What is the significance of the imagery of the "gates" here,
    as pointed out in the video?

3. What was Jesus' method of defeating Satan, sin, and phys-
    ical death—the "gates of Hades"? (See Matthew 16:21–23;
    1 Corinthians 15:26–28.)

4. What is the source of our power to confront evil? (See Eph-
    esians 1:17–23; Acts 1:8; 19:20; Luke 10:17–19; Ephesians
    6:10–18; Hebrews 4:12.)

Topic D: Dead Gods Versus the Living God

When the Israelites entered Canaan, they found a land of farmers who
attributed their fertile land to their god, Baal. So the Jews struggled,
wondering whether to worship the God who had guided them to the
Promised Land, or to honor the fertility god of the land, or to worship both. Today God's people still face the struggle: will we be totally
committed to God or will we honor the "gods" of the places we
inhabit?

1. What is the difference between the living God and idols
    such as Pan, the fertility god worshiped in Caesarea
    Philippi? (See Jeremiah 10:1–16.)

2. Read the following passages and note the ways in which God demonstrated His supremacy over Baal.

Reference	God's Power Demonstrated
Joshua 3:9–17	
Judges 5:19–21	
1 Kings 17:1; 18:1, 21–45	
2 Kings 2:8, 11–14, 19–22	

3. Impatient to receive their place to live in the Promised Land, the tribe of Dan refused to remain in the territory God had provided and established the city of Dan on Israel's northern border.

   a. For what was the city of Dan known? (See Judges 18:1–2, 23–31; 1 Kings 12:25–31.)

   b. What was the fate of the city of Dan? (See 1 Kings 15:20.)

4. What are some of the "gods" that are worshiped in our cul-
    ture? In what ways do these gods contrast with the true,
    living God?

5. In what ways do you see the community of Christians sim-
    ply coexisting with, rather than confronting, the "gods" of
    this world?

IDENTITY PROFILE

Who Was Baal?

- The fertility god of the Canaanites.
- Believed to be the supreme god because he had defeated the sea god
  and so controlled the sea and could prevent storms.
- Believed to have power over weather.
- Often depicted as a man with the head and horns of a bull, carrying a
  lightning bolt in his hand(s).
- Attractive to his followers because of his supposed ability to provide
  rain in a dry country.
- Supposedly went to the land of the dead, the underworld, each year
  and returned to bring rain to the earth and create abundant harvests.
- Appeased through sacrifices, usually animals (1 Kings 18:23), although
  Baal's followers sometimes, during times of crisis, sacrificed their children (Deuteronomy 12:31; 18:9–11).
- Thought to have a mistress, Asherah—the fertility goddess. Believing
  that the sexual union of Baal and Asherah produced fertility, pagan
  worshipers engaged in immoral sex to cause the gods to join together
  and ensure good harvests.

faith Lesson

Time for Reflection

The following passage of Scripture recounts the discussion Jesus had with His disciples concerning His identity. Read this passage silently and take a few minutes to consider who you believe Jesus to be.

> When Jesus came to the region of Caesarea Philippi, he asked his disciples, "Who do people say the Son of Man is?" They replied, "Some say John the Baptist; others say Elijah; and still others, Jeremiah or one of the prophets." "But what about you?" he asked. "Who do you say I am?" Simon Peter answered, "You are the Christ, the Son of the living God." Jesus replied, "Blessed are you, Simon son of Jonah, for this was not revealed to you by man, but by my Father in heaven. And I tell you that you are Peter, and on this rock I will build my church, and the gates of Hades will not overcome it.". . . From that time on Jesus began to explain to his disciples that he must go to Jerusalem and suffer many things at the hands of the elders, chief priests and teachers of the law, and that he must be killed and on the third day be raised to life. Peter took him aside and began to rebuke him. "Never, Lord!" he said. "This shall never happen to you!" Jesus turned and said to Peter, "Get behind me, Satan! You are a stumbling block to me; you do not have in mind the things of God, but the things of men." Then Jesus said to his disciples, "If anyone would come after me, he must deny himself and take up his cross and follow me. For whoever wants to save his life will lose it, but whoever loses his life for me will find it. What good will it be for a man if he gains the whole world, yet forfeits his soul? Or what can a man give in exchange for his soul?"
>
> MATTHEW 16:13–18, 21–26

1. Have you come to the point in your life when you, like Peter, have said with conviction, "You are the Christ, the Son of the living God"? What impact does that belief have

on your life? In what ways should that belief have a greater impact on your life? Be specific.

2. Where do you see the "gates of Hades" most clearly in your community? In what ways are you seeking opportunities to confront Satan's power?

3. In what ways are you tempted to hide from, rather than challenge, evil? Which steps are you willing to take in order to challenge evil in Jesus' name? Be specific.

THE TRUTH OF THE MATTER

To believe in Jesus (*Yeshua*) is to accept His work of saving sinners from sin and to accept the mission to take on the gates of hell. To believe in Christ (Messiah, *Mashiach*) is to confess that He was chosen and equipped by God for His office as prophet, priest, and king. Jesus accomplished the task he was sent to do by serving others and suffering for them, even unto death. Following Christ means accepting His command to suffer for Him and to serve others on His behalf. When we engage in the process of believing and following, we are truly Christian (Christlike).

4. Which specific form of evil might God be calling you to confront within your sphere of influence? What sacrifices might be required of you to challenge that evil? Are you prepared to pay that cost?

5. Do you know people who are effectively challenging the evil of this world? If so, what can you learn from them and apply to your own life?

Action Points

Take a moment to review the key points you explored today. Then write down the action step (or steps) that you will commit to this week as a result of what you have discovered.

1. *As Jesus taught His disciples in Caesarea Philippi, He said that they were to challenge the most pagan expressions of the power of evil.* He assured them that on that "rock"— the place where Satan is strongest in society, where ungodly values and beliefs are boldly promoted—He would build His church.

2. *Jesus' message applies to the followers of Jesus—the church—today, just as it did to His disciples in Caesarea Philippi.* We are to go on the offensive and actively confront the "gates of Hades." In the power of God, we are to challenge anything that is not godly—through our attitudes, words, and actions. We can gain confidence from

Jesus' promise to His disciples that the power of evil, the "gates of Hades," cannot prevail against the church of Jesus the Messiah.

I will prepare myself and actively use _____

_____

(the gifts, abilities, and opportunities God has given me)

to challenge_____
                    (the evil within my sphere of influence)

in the name and power of Jesus.

In the power of Christ, we can bring His message to people who are not Christians and also confront evil around us. The following Scripture passage offers encouragement as we seek to challenge evil in our world:

> I write to you, dear children, because your sins have been forgiven on account of his name. . . . I write to you, fathers, because you have known him who is from the beginning. I write to you, young men, because you are strong, and the word of God lives in you, and you have overcome the evil one.

> 1 JOHN 2:12, 14

city of the great king— the temple

questions to think about

1. When you think about the great cities you have visited or in which you have lived, what thoughts come to mind? What do those cities inspire in you in relationship to history, human accomplishment (or failure), human nature, etc.?

2. When you think of Jerusalem, what thoughts come to mind?

3. In what ways have events in Jerusalem affected our Christian faith?

video notes

The Topography of Jerusalem

The Temple Mount

Events Within the Temple

A House of Prayer for All Nations

video Highlights

On the diagram of the city of Jerusalem during Jesus' time, note the location of the Temple Mount, the Royal Stoa, and David's City on the slope below.

1. How have your impressions of Jerusalem changed as a result of seeing this video?

2. Why was the temple in Jerusalem so important to the Jews during Jesus' time?

3. Why is it so significant that the temple even had a court for lepers?

4. Imagine yourself as one of the Sadducean priests who operated the temple and consider what you might have thought and how you might have responded when Jesus forced the buyers and sellers out of the temple.

Jerusalem of Jesus' Time

1 Temple Mount
2 Temple
3 Antonia
4 Hasmonaean Palace
5 Herod's Palace
6 Theater
7 First Wall
8 Second Wall
9 David's City
10 Lower City
11 Upper City
12 Business District
13 Garden Gate
14 Towers (Damascus)
   Gate

15 Kidron Valley
16 Tyropoeon Valley
17 Golden Gate
18 Southern Stairs
19 South Wall
20 Royal Stoa
21 Opening of Entrance
   Tunnels on Temple
   Mount
22 Robinson's Arch
23 Barclay's Gate
24 Wilson's Arch &
   Bridge
25 Warren's Gate

26 Tadi Gate
27 Pool of Bethesda
28 Eastern Gate
29 Double Gates
30 Triple Gates
31 Hinnom Valley
32 Essene Quarter
33 Mansions
34 Entrance to Antonia
35 New City
36 Golgotha (?)
37 Garden Tomb

small group Bible Discovery

Topic A: The Importance of Mount Moriah

1. For what reason did Abraham travel to the region of Moriah? What happened there? (See Genesis 22:1–14.)

2. Describe how David, after receiving a prophetic word from Gad—his prophet—selected the future site of the temple on Mount Moriah. How did God confirm His approval of the site? (See 1 Chronicles 21:18–26; 22:1.)

3. What did David bring into his city on Mount Moriah? (See 2 Samuel 6:1–5.)

Jerusalem of David and Soloman

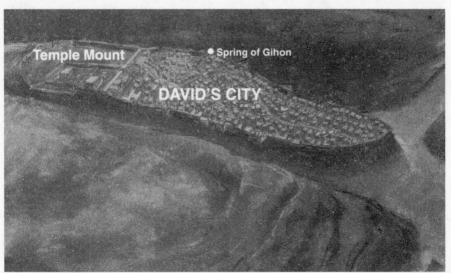

4. Whom did God select to build the temple? What kind of a temple did he build, and where did he begin building it? (See 1 Chronicles 28:2–7; 2 Chronicles 2:5; 3:1.)

5. Which other important historical event took place near Jerusalem and Mount Moriah? (See Matthew 27:32–35.)

6. What common thread links Abraham's experience on Mount Moriah, the Israelites' offering of sacrifices there, and Jesus' crucifixion?

PROFILES IN CONTRAST	
Herod the Great	**Jesus**
Built spectacular buildings: the temple in Jerusalem; Masada, a fortress in the Judea Wilderness; Jericho; and the seaport in Caesarea.	Built with people—living stones (Matthew 16:18; 1 Peter 2:4–8).
Built to honor himself.	Built for the honor of God.
His works lie in ruins today.	His projects will last forever.

The Temple Mount: A.D. 70

1 Temple
2 Royal Stoa
3 Soloman's Colonnade
4 Southern Stairs
5 South Wall

6 Double Gates
7 Triple Gates
8 Ritual Baths
9 Plaza
10 Robinson's Arch

11 Barclay's Gate
12 Wilson's Arch
13 Warren's Gate
14 Place of Trumpeting
15 Tyropoeon Street

Topic B: God's Presence Among His People

1. What did God promise Solomon regarding the temple? (See 1 Kings 6:11–13.)

2. At the dedication of the temple, what did the priests place in the temple? How did God reveal His presence in the temple? (See 1 Kings 8:6,10–11; 2 Chronicles 5:11–6:2; 7:1–3.)

3. In which other situations has God revealed His presence through fire? (See Exodus 19:17–18; 24:15–18; 1 Kings 18:22–24, 36–38; 1 Chronicles 21:25–26; Revelation 1:9–15.)

4. Jewish people consistently came into the temple to be in the presence of God. Read the following passages of Scripture and note the sentiment expressed:

Scripture	Sentiment
Psalm 15	
Psalm 27:4	
Psalm 99:1–3	
Psalm 122:1, 9	
Isaiah 6	
Isaiah 37:14–20	

DATA FILE

Solomon's Temple

Construction began about 950 B.C. on the Mount Moriah site chosen by David at God's leading—on a high point of the ridge known as David's City, just north of the original city.

- Construction took seven years.
- No hammers or chisels were used on the site; the stones were prepared at the quarry.
- Made of limestone, parts of which were covered with gold and cedar.
- It was precisely and luxuriously furnished (1 Kings 7:13–51; 2 Chronicles 4).
- It held the Ark of the Covenant (1 Kings 8:1–21; 2 Chronicles 5).
- After its dedication to God (1 Kings 8:22–66; 2 Chronicles 6), the temple was filled by God's presence (2 Chronicles 5:13–14; 7:1–3).

The First Temple at Jerusalem

5. After Jesus' death and resurrection, during the Jewish feast of Pentecost, what represented God's presence as it moved from the temple building into the new temple—the disciples? (See Acts 2:1–3.)

6. At one time, God's presence resided in the Holy of Holies in the temple (2 Chronicles 5:7). Where does God's presence dwell today? (See 1 Corinthians 3:16–17; 6:19.)

DATA FILE

Herod's Building of the Temple

Made of marble and gold, Herod's Temple was taller than a fifteen-story building. The temple platform—the largest temple base in the ancient world—was more than 900 feet wide from east to west and more than 1,500 feet long from north to south. Built on the exact location of Solomon's temple and the temple Nehemiah reconstructed, it could accommodate hundreds of thousands of pilgrims at a time and was twice as large as the largest temple enclosure in Rome.

A thousand priests trained as masons by Herod worked on the temple, as did ten thousand highly skilled laborers using a thousand wagons. Some limestone blocks of the supporting platform weigh more than five hundred tons.

The Eastern Wall followed the original line dating from Solomon's days. The main feature in the wall, the Eastern Gate, was the original eastern entrance to Temple Mount. At one point, the walls of the temple rose more than 225 feet above the bottom of the Kidron Valley.

The South Wall was more than 900 feet long and more than 150 feet high. Pilgrims entered the temple primarily through this entrance—the Double Gates—after climbing the Southern Stairs—a broad staircase more than 200 feet wide.

The Western Wall was a common gathering place during Jesus' time and featured various architectural wonders and gates, such as:

- *Robinson's Arch*—one of the largest masonry arches (75 feet tall, more than 45 feet across) in the ancient world; supported a massive staircase that ran from the Tyropoeon Valley and the Lower City to the Royal Stoa (the place of buying and selling, the location of the temple treasury, and the Sanhedrin's meeting place); destroyed in A.D. 70 by the Romans.
- *Barclay's Gate*—provided access to the Gentile Court from Tyropoeon Street.
- *Wilson's Arch*—supported a bridge that extended from the Upper City, where the Sadducees and other influential Jews lived, across the Tyropoeon Valley to the Temple Mount; extended 75 feet above the valley floor and spanned 45 feet.
- *Warren's Gate*—provided direct access to the temple courts.
- *Massive Ashlars*—hand-shaped stones brought from a quarry nearly a mile away. One 45-foot-long stone weighs nearly 600 tons. (See Mark 13:1–2; Luke 21:5.)

The North Wall is where the Antonia fortress was located. Built by Herod the Great, this fortress guarded the northern side of Jerusalem and held Roman troops during Jesus' time who watched the temple activities. Paul was probably brought to the Antonia after his arrest and defended himself on the stairs that apparently led to the fortress (Acts 21:27–40; 22:22–25).

The temple platform's extension to the west required enormous retaining walls on the south and west. Some of the rocks used in the wall weighed more than five hundred tons each. The finished platform was divided into courts, which became increasingly more sacred the closer they were to the temple.

Artist's rendering of Herod's Temple

1	Holy of Holies	4	Altar	7	Holy Place
2	Altar of Incense	5	Porch	8	Veil
3	Table of Showbread	6	Bronze Sea	9	Menorah

Topic C: Events That Occurred in the Temple Courts

1. How often did Jesus teach in the temple courts? How was His message received?

Reference	Teaching/Reception
Matthew 26:55	
Mark 11:27–28	
Mark 12:35–37	
Luke 2:41–47	
John 7:14–16	
John 8:2–11	
John 10:22–33	

2. Why do you think Jesus spent so much time teaching in the temple courts?

3. Where did the early Christians meet and teach? What can we learn from the fact that they met and taught there? (See Acts 2:44–46; 5:17–21.)

4. Where did Peter heal a man who had been crippled since birth? (See Acts 3:1–16, refer to diagram of the Temple Courts on page 74.)

   a. Whose example did Peter follow? (See John 5:1–14.)

BACKGROUND NOTES

The Pharisees

- Derived their name from the word *perushim*, which meant "separated" or "separatists."
- Tried to be devoted to God without resorting to violence against the Romans.
- Devoted themselves to obeying every detail of Jewish law and separating themselves from all influences or people who might interfere with that devotion.
- Believed that Moses had given a two-part law—the written law of the Torah and additional oral commandments that had been passed through generations to help the faithful understand and apply the written law.
- The Pharisees interpreted and greatly expanded the oral law, which became a complex guide to everyday life. Their intent was to help people understand the Torah, in much the same way that Christians use a creed or catechism to help summarize and interpret the Bible.
- Believed in the physical resurrection of the dead, a coming day of judgment, the coming of the Messiah, angels, and a loving God who desired a life of obedience.
- Recognized a combination of free choice and divine control in human life.
- Had some people within their ranks who were hypocritical or became so focused on obedience that they did not notice or care about the needs of other people. Jesus never criticized anyone for being a Pharisee and instructed His followers to obey what the Pharisees taught

(Matthew 23:2–3). Jesus only criticized "hypocritical" ones (Matthew 23) and those who spoiled the whole group (Matthew 16:6,11). In fact, many Pharisees supported Jesus, tried to protect Him (Luke 13:31), and became Jesus' followers (Acts 15:5).
- Obtained their authority by knowledge and piety.

The Sadducees
- After Israel returned from the Babylonian captivity, it was the tradition that the high priest must be from the tribe of Levi, the family of Aaron, and the family of Zadok—Solomon's high priest (1 Kings 2:35; Ezekiel 40:46). Descendants of this family, *Zedukim* (or "Sadducee" in English), were the temple authorities throughout the time before Jesus was born. Descendants of Zadok and their supporters were also called "Sadducees."
- Although there may have been fewer than a thousand of them, they wielded great power.
- Were wealthy, politically active, and had a majority in the Sanhedrin— the religious council used by the Romans and Herods as the instrument to govern the Jewish people.
- Controlled the economy of the temple, often using their position for personal gain (Mark 11:15–18). In A.D. 15, they allowed the business of buying and selling to extend beyond the Royal Stoa and into the Gentile Court, a move which the Pharisees opposed.
- Many were Hellenistic but faithful to temple rituals.
- Believed the written Torah alone was authoritative, rejected oral law, hated the Pharisees, denied bodily resurrection and most Pharisaic doctrines of angels and spirits, and believed that the synagogue and study of the Torah as a form of worship undermined temple ritual.
- Obtained their authority by position and birth.
- Frequently dealt brutally with anyone who undermined the temple, its economy (their income), and its ritual.
- Had the most to lose because of Jesus. Any popular movement jeopardized their place as the majority in the Sanhedrin and the support of the Romans who ruled through it (John 11:49–53).
- Ceased to exist as a group after the temple in Jerusalem was destroyed.

Topic D: The Temple—a House of Prayer for All Nations

At the southern end of the temple platform was a beautiful colonnade named the Royal Stoa (see diagram of the Temple Mount A.D. 70 on page 79). It had a central hall, 162 large columns, and by Jesus' time had become the area where transactions for temple sacrifices took place. However, the booths for buying and selling sacrifices, the inspection of animals, and the changing of foreign currencies—all of which were operated by Sadducean priests—overflowed into the Gentile Court, which was the large, open area around the sacred temple courts where Gentiles were allowed to worship (see diagram of the Temple Courts on page 74). These activities apparently interfered with the Gentiles' worship of the one true God.

1. Describe what Jesus did in the Royal Stoa after His triumphant entry into Jerusalem (Matthew 21:12–13; Luke 19:45; John 2:13–17).

2. According to Isaiah 56:7, the Scripture Jesus quoted when He drove out the vendors and money changers, what was God's "house" to be called?

3. Why did Jesus drive the vendors and money changers out of the temple? (See Matthew 21:13.)

The Temple Courts

4. What truth did Jesus demonstrate by clearing out the Gentile Court?

5. What can we learn from the fact that Jesus expressed great anger toward religious leaders who didn't care about hurting, sinful, broken people and "unclean" Gentiles? What might we be doing today that would kindle Jesus' anger in a similar way?

Topic E: The Soreq—and Other Dividing Walls Within the Temple

The *Soreq* was a five-foot-tall stone wall that surrounded the inner courts of the consecrated temple area and was designed to keep Gentiles and other "unacceptable" people out of the inner courts. Gentiles could not pass the Soreq on pain of death.

1. What was Paul accused of doing? (See Acts 21:27–35.)

2. Later, in Ephesians 2:14, what did Paul say had been destroyed? When he used that phrase, what others kinds of "walls" might he have been describing?

3. In light of the previous question, if Paul were alive today which walls might he point out to us that divide us from other people?

4. What can you do to break down walls that divide you from other people?

5. In addition to the Soreq, there were a number of other walls and divisions within the temple. Identify the separation indicated by each of the following (refer to the diagram of the Temple Courts on page 74):

Area of the Temple	Type of Separation
The Court of the Women	
Chamber of Nazirites	
Chamber of Lepers	
Court of the Israelites	
Court of the Priests	
Sanctuary of the Temple	
The Holy of Holies	

faith Lesson

Time for Reflection

The following passages of Scripture provide a glimpse of how God viewed His temple. Read these passages silently and consider the importance of God's temple and how the message of the temple applies to your life.

> "And foreigners who bind themselves to the LORD to serve him, to love the name of the LORD, and to worship him, all who keep the Sabbath without desecrating it and who hold fast to my covenant—these I will bring to my holy mountain and give them joy in my house of prayer. Their burnt offerings and sacrifices will be accepted on my altar; for my house will be called a house of prayer for all nations."
>
> ISAIAH 56:6–7

> On reaching Jerusalem, Jesus entered the temple area and began driving out those who were buying and selling there. He overturned the tables of the money changers and the benches of those selling doves, and would not allow anyone to carry merchandise through the temple courts. And as he taught them, he said, "Is it not written: "'My house will be called a house of prayer for all nations'? But you have made it 'a den of robbers.'" The chief priests and the teachers of the law heard this and began looking for a way to kill him, for they feared him, because the whole crowd was amazed at his teaching.
>
> MARK 11:15–18

> Meanwhile, the high priest questioned Jesus about his disciples and his teaching. "I have spoken openly to the world," Jesus replied. "I always taught in synagogues or at the temple, where all the Jews come together. I said nothing in secret. Why question me? Ask those who heard me. Surely they know what I said." When Jesus said this,

one of the officials nearby struck him in the face. "Is this the way you answer the high priest?" he demanded. "If I said something wrong," Jesus replied, "testify as to what is wrong. But if I spoke the truth, why did you strike me?" Then Annas sent him, still bound, to Caiaphas the high priest.

JOHN 18:19–24

1. In light of what the temple symbolized for the Jews, what have you learned about the character of God and the relationship He desires to have with us?

2. Now that you've learned more about the ancient temple, what insights have you gained into why Jesus drove out the money changers? Into why the Sadducees wanted to kill Him?

3. In what ways has understanding the power of the temple leaders and the might of the Roman empire helped you understand the commitment Jesus had to communicating God's truth—no matter what the cost?

Development of the Temple Mount

Hasmonaean Expansion

Herod's Expansion

50m   0

A Chronology of Temple Events

Approx. 2,000 B.C. Abraham was sent to the Moriah area to sacrifice Isaac. Jerusalem was later built on the mountain named Moriah.

Approx. 1,000 B.C. David captured the Canaanite city of Jebus (2 Samuel 5:6–7) and named it the City of David, which he made his capital (1 Chronicles 11:7). He selected the temple site on the threshing floor of Araunah on Mount Moriah, where he built an altar.

Approx. 950 B.C. Solomon built the temple on the Mount Moriah site chosen by David at God's leading. After the Ark of the Covenant—the resting place of God's glorious presence—was moved into the temple—God's earthly home—the people prayed for God's presence (2 Chronicles 6) and God sent fire to consume their sacrifices (2 Chronicles 7:1–3).

586 B.C. The Babylonians destroyed the temple and took many Israelites captive.

Approx. 500 B.C. Cyrus, king of Persia, decreed that the Israelites could return to Jerusalem. Under Ezra and Nehemiah's leadership, the temple was rebuilt (Ezra 1:1–4; 3:7–13; 6:15). Since there was no Ark of the Covenant, the Holy of Holies was left empty. The Jews rejoiced when the Torah was read (Nehemiah 8:17).

322 B.C. Jerusalem, rebuilt during Ezra's time, became part of Alexander the Great's empire. The city suffered more than a century of conflict at the hands of Alexander's Hellenistic successors. Antiochus, the king of the Syrians, outlawed the Sabbath, circumcision, the study of Torah, and even defiled the great altar by sacrificing pigs on it.

165 B.C. The Maccabean revolt against the Greek army brought Jerusalem back under Jewish control. The menorah—the symbol of eternal light in the Holy of

Holies—was relit. Descendants of the Maccabees expanded the Temple Mount. The city now covered 175 acres and had more than 30,000 inhabitants.

63 B.C.	The Romans take control of Judea.
37–4 B.C.	Herod, the king of Israel appointed by Rome, lavishly expanded the Temple Mount, embellished the temple, fortified the city, and built many spectacular buildings. A wonder of the ancient world, the city was now ready for the ministry of Jesus, the Messiah. But Herod also conducted a reign of terror designed to keep the Jewish people in line. To keep his position, Herod needed the might of Rome, the support of the Sadducees (the temple authorities), and the favor of Hellenistic Jews. Afraid of losing his throne to the Messiah, Herod killed the male babies in Bethlehem (Matthew 2:16).
Approx. A.D. 30	The Sadducees had Jesus crucified. The Holy Spirit came upon the disciples in the temple courts; the veil separating the inner chamber of the temple (the Holy of Holies) split from top to bottom, symbolizing the access all believers now had to God's presence through Jesus. On the Christian fulfillment of Pentecost, God took up residence in a new temple—His community of believers (1 Corinthians 3:16–17).
A.D. 44	Herod Agrippa I, grandson of Herod the Great, died. Rebel Jews began killing Romans and Jews who cooperated with them, and Roman governors became increasingly cruel. The temple priesthood became more dependent on the Romans for security and support and became more corrupt.
A.D. 66	A Gentile offered a "pagan" sacrifice next to the synagogue's entrance in Caesarea. The Jerusalem authorities decided to end all foreign sacrifices. The Rome-appointed governor, Florus, authorized Roman troops to raid the temple treasury. When the Jews protested, Florus's troops killed many innocent civilians.

In turn, Jewish mobs drove out the Roman troops, stormed the Antonia (the Roman fort), and occupied the fortress of Masada. When the Romans in Caesarea learned what had happened, they killed 20,000 Jews within a day's time.

A.D. 68
Ultra-nationalistic Jews (the Zealots) appointed their own temple priest and slaughtered the Sadducee priests who resisted.

A.D. 70
Under Titus, at least 80,000 Roman troops destroyed Jerusalem, slaughtering hundreds of thousands of Jews. The streets ran with Jewish blood. On August 9, the temple was burned and destroyed. All the citizens of Jerusalem (more than one million) were executed, sold into slavery, or captured for games in the arena.

A.D. 131
A second Jewish revolt started, driving Christianity to the ends of the earth, where it soon became a largely Gentile faith. Only today are the Jewish roots of Christianity being fully appreciated.

A.D. 135
Rome squashed the second revolt, outlawed the Jewish religion, and Judea became Palestine. Rabbinic Judaism became the Orthodox faith of Jewish people today. The Jews became a people without a country.

Action Points

Take a moment to review the key points you explored today. Then write down the action step (or steps) you will commit to this week as a result of what you have discovered.

1. *Learning about the temple in Jerusalem—its structures, practices, history—gives us insight into the heart of God and His desire to bring salvation to His people.* It also helps us visualize biblical events that occurred in Jerusalem.

   What will you do to continue to learn the ways in which the Christian faith is rooted in Jewish culture?

2. *God wanted His temple—the symbol of His presence on earth—to be available to everyone.* He designated it to be a house of prayer for all nations—Jews, Gentiles, even lepers. Ray Vander Laan believes that's why Jesus became so angry when the temple authorities allowed vendors to carry on their trade in the Court of the Gentiles, which would disrupt the Gentiles who had come to worship God.

   In what ways might you be insensitive to the spiritual needs of other people around you, just as the temple authorities were insensitive to the Gentiles by allowing merchandise to be bought and sold in the area set aside for their worship?

What steps will you take to broaden your horizons and invite people who are presently outside the church, outside the community of believers, to come in and discover and worship God?

city of the great king— Jerusalem

questions to think about

1. Think for a moment about the times you have explored great historical sites—perhaps the U.S. capitol building, or White House, the site of the Battle of Gettysburg, the Great Wall of China, the great castles of Europe, the pyramids of Egypt, etc.—or viewed a reenactment of a great event. Consider for a moment what life was like for people who lived through the significant events of those places. Consider what life would have been like for you in those places.

2. Consider what you know about the sights, sounds, fears, hopes, joys, and heartaches of the people of Jerusalem in Jesus' day.

video notes

Features of the City Districts

Herod's Palace

The Jewish Mansion

The Antonia

Jesus: Our Scapegoat

video Highlights

On the map of Jerusalem (page 88) note the various districts of the city and the locations of the Mount of Olives, the Temple Mount, the Eastern Gate, Herod's Palace, the Jewish mansions, the Antonia, and the Garden Gate.

1. In our previous session, we explored the ancient temple and learned quite a bit about the Jews' religious practices, temple history, and Jesus' ministry in the temple. Today, we looked at other historical sites in Jerusalem. In what ways have you gained a better understanding of what life was like during Jesus' day?

2. Explain what you think it would have been like to have been an ordinary Jewish person who lived in a city ruled by the temple authorities, Herod, and the Romans.

3. What did you feel as you saw what Herod's palace looked like—and realized that the wise men and Jesus had probably been there?

4.   What surprised you as you learned about the mansion that was probably owned by one of the Jewish high priests?

5.   In what ways does Jerusalem, which has experienced more than three thousand years of history, inspire you?

Jerusalem's Districts

A	David's City	1	Eastern Gate	8	Antonia	15	Golgotha (?)	21	Essence Quarter
B	New City	2	Southern Gate	9	Tadi Gate	16	Garden Tomb	22	Mansions
C	Upper City	3	Royal Stoa	10	Pool of Bethesda	17	Spring of Gihon	23	Mount of Olives
D	Business District	4	Robinson's Arch	11	First Wall	18	Hinnom Valley	24	Kidron Valley
E	Temple Mount	5	Wilson's Arch	12	Second Wall	19	Theatre	25	Huldah Gates
F	Lower City	6	Tyropoeon Street	13	Garden Gate	20	Citadel and		
G	Herod's Palace	7	Warren's Gate	14	Towers (Damascus) Gate		Herod's palace		

DATA FILE

The Geographic Features and Events of Jerusalem

Hinnom Valley formed the western boundary of the Western Hill and the Upper City of Jesus' time; began along the Western Hill and ended where the Tyropoeon and Kidron Valleys met.

Location where the kings and people of Judah sacrificed their children to Baal (2 Kings 23:10; 2 Chronicles 28:3–4; 33:1, 6; Jeremiah 7:31; 19:5–6; 32:35) and where Jerusalem's garbage was burned; became a synonym for hell itself (Matthew 5:22, 29; 10:28; 18:9; 23:33; Mark 9:43–48; James 3:6).

Kidron Valley, a deep wadi about three miles long, east of the city between David's city and the Mount of Olives.

David crossed here when fleeing Absalom (2 Samuel 15:13–24); various kings destroyed idols and pagan objects here (1 Kings 15:11–12; 2 Kings 23:4–7, 12–14; 2 Chronicles 15:16); Jesus crossed here on his way

Topography of Jerusalem

to Gethsemane just before His arrest (John 18:1); Joel prophesied concerning the judgment of nations in the Valley of Jehoshaphat—believed to be part or all of this valley (Joel 3:2, 12); and Solomon refused to allow Shimei to cross here (1 Kings 2:36–38). Hezekiah's tunnel brought fresh water from the Spring of Gihon, which was in the valley, to the Pool of Siloam.

Mount of Olives, the highest peak in the area.

David went here to escape Absalom's revolt (2 Samuel 15:13–37); Jesus entered Jerusalem from here (Matthew 21:1–11; Luke 19:1, 28–44), gave His final teaching here (Matthew 24:3–46), and ascended to heaven from here (Luke 24:50–52; Acts 1:6–12). May be the location for Jesus' return (Zechariah 14:4; Acts 1:11).

Tyropoeon Valley, between David's City and the Western Hill where the Upper City was located.

Hezekiah expanded the city into this valley; the western wall of Herod's Gentile Court was located here, as was the Pool of Siloam where Jesus sent a blind man to wash (John 9:1–12); Nehemiah repaired the wall near the Pool of Siloam (Nehemiah 3:15).

Western Hill, now called Mount Zion, was called the "Upper City" during Jesus' time.

The site of Herod's palace; probably where the wise men talked with Herod the Great (Matthew 2:1–7), Herod Antipas met Jesus (Luke 23:6–7), and where the Upper Room was located (Luke 22:7–13; Acts 1:12–13).

small Group Bible Discovery

Topic A: God Preserves His Holy City

During King Hezekiah's reign over Judah, he prepared for attack by Assyria, a pagan nation that in 722 B.C. destroyed the northern kingdom of Israel.

1. What kind of a king was Hezekiah? (See 2 Chronicles 29:1–3, 35–36; 31:1, 20–21.)

2. What did Assyria do during the fourteenth year of King Hezekiah's reign? (See Isaiah 36:1; 2 Kings 18:13.)

3. What had Hezekiah done to prepare for the Assyrian attack against Jerusalem? (See 1 Kings 20:20; 2 Chronicles 32:1–5.)

4. How did Hezekiah respond upon receiving the Assyrians' ultimatum? (See Isaiah 37:14–20.)

5. How did God deliver His people? (See 2 Chronicles 32:20–23.)

6. As we consider how God saved Jerusalem, what lessons can we learn about God and the problems we face today?

Topic B: Jesus Heals at the Pool of Bethesda

Refer to the map of Jerusalem on page 88 and locate the Sheep Gate (also called Tadi Gate) on Jerusalem's northern wall. Just north of the gate is the Pool of Bethesda, which was believed to have healing powers.

1. Who would come to the pool and why? (See John 5:1–7.)

2. When Jesus came to the pool, what was his response? What did He do? (See John 5:6–9.)

3. What did the man do? How do we know that he didn't know who Jesus was? (See John 5:11–13.)

DATA FILE

The Development of Jerusalem

2,000 B.C. God sends Abraham to the area of Mount Moriah to sacrifice
(circa) Isaac. (The temple and part of Jerusalem is built on the mountain ridge named Moriah.)

1,000 B.C. David captures Jerusalem (then the Canaanite city of Jebus),
(circa) names it the City of David, and makes it his capital (2 Samuel 5:6–7; 1 Chronicles 11:4–7). The city is about ten acres in size and is home to 1,500 people.

950 B.C. Solomon spends seven years building the temple, then spends
(circa) thirteen years building his lavish palace (1 Kings 6:37–7:12), apparently between the temple and David's City. The city has about 4,500 people and covers approximately thirty acres.

700 B.C. Hezekiah expands Jerusalem—west across the Tyropoeon
(circa) Valley onto the Western Hill—and fortifies the city against the Babylonian threat by building walls and tearing down houses in order to expand the walls (2 Chronicles 32:1–5; Isaiah 22:10). The city at that time covered about 100 acres and housed 24,000 people.

500 B.C. The Babylonians capture Jerusalem, destroy the temple, and
(circa) take many Israelites captive.

430 B.C. Cyrus, king of Persia, allows the Israelites to return to Jerusalem.
(circa) They rebuild the temple and restore and dedicate the city walls (Nehemiah 2:1–8; 3; 12:27–47).

322 B.C. Jerusalem becomes part of Alexander the Great's empire. The city suffers more than a century of conflict at the hands of Alexander's successors.

165 B.C. The Maccabean revolt brings Jerusalem back under Jewish control. Descendants of the Maccabees enclose the Western Hill, build the fortress Baris (later the Antonia), and expand the Gentile Court. The city now covers 175 acres and has more than 30,000 inhabitants.

63 B.C.	The Romans under Pompey capture Jerusalem from the Hasmonaeans (Maccabean descendants) and eventually place the city and country under Herod's control.
37–4 B.C.	Herod the Great expands the Gentile Court, lavishly embellishes the temple, fortifies the city, and builds many structures. A wonder of the ancient world, the city has expanded to nearly 250 acres and has a population of 45,000.
A.D. 70	Under Titus, at least 80,000 Roman troops destroy Jerusalem, slaughtering hundreds of thousands of Jews. The streets run with Jewish blood. On August 9, the temple is burned and destroyed. All the citizens of Jerusalem (more than one million) are executed, sold into slavery, or captured for games in the arena.

4. After being healed, where did the man go? Why do you think he went there? (See John 5:8–9, 14.)

5. If you feel comfortable doing so, share a time when you experienced an unusual blessing from God that at first you did not realize came from Him.

6. When God provides for us in miraculous ways, what messages do you think He is trying to convey? (See John 5:6, 8–9, 14.)

Topic C: Jesus Heals in the Lower City

Refer to the map of Jerusalem on page 88 and locate the Lower City.

1. During Jesus' day, the Lower City was home to most of the common people. What had King Hezekiah done years earlier to bring fresh water into this part of the city? (See 2 Kings 20:20; 2 Chronicles 32:30.)

2. What happened at the Pool of Siloam, which was located in the Lower City and filled by the water flowing through Hezekiah's tunnel? (See John 9:1–12.)

3. Apparently the blind man mentioned in the previous question was near the temple when Jesus saw him (John 8:58– 9:1). In order to reach the Pool of Siloam, he would have had to work his way down many steps. Why do you think Jesus put mud on the man's eyes and then asked him to walk down such a long, difficult path?

4. Jesus required the blind man to demonstrate faith and obedience, which resulted in his healing. In what way(s) does God ask us to demonstrate our faith and obedience when He accomplishes His work in our lives?

5. Why is it important for us, like the blind man mentioned
    in John 9:1–12, to step out in faith when we ask God to
    work in and through us?

Topic D: Jesus Creates a Stir in the Upper City

Herod built his palace in the Upper City, which was located on the
Western Hill (today called Mount Zion) in the highest section of
Jerusalem. The palace, which covered nearly five acres, had beautiful
gardens, fountains, and accommodations for hundreds of guests. In
the vicinity of the palace are several mansions that are believed to have
been the homes of priestly families and wealthy nobility. Although the
Romans burned these houses in A.D. 70, evidence of their splendor
remains. They help us picture the wealth of the Jewish religious leaders, who were so threatened by Jesus that they wanted to have Him
killed.

1. When was the news of the arrival of Jesus, King of the
    Jews, first heard in the Upper City? How did the people of
    that district respond? (See Matthew 2:1–12, 16–18.)

2. After Jesus raised Lazarus from the dead (John 11:38–44),
    what did the chief priests and religious leaders who lived in
    the mansions in the Upper City do? (See John 11:45–53.)

DATA FILE

The Districts of Jerusalem
To locate these districts, please refer to the map of Jerusalem on page 88.

David's City: The Jerusalem of David's time, located on a narrow strip of land (Mount Moriah) about ten acres in size, populated by about 1,500 people, naturally defended by the Kidron Valley to the east and the Tyropoeon Valley to the west, originally named Zion, received fresh water from the Spring of Gihon.

Events that happened here: Abraham brought Isaac to Mount Moriah to sacrifice him (Genesis 22:1–2,14); the Philistines returned the Ark of the Covenant (1 Samuel 6:1–2, 12–16); and David purchased the threshing floor of Araunah, which became the site of the temple (2 Samuel 24:18–25); Solomon built the temple on Mount Moriah (2 Chronicles 3:1–2); David was tempted and committed adultery with Bathsheba (2 Samuel 11:2–5); Michal, David's wife, saw him dancing joyfully before the Lord and "despised him" (1 Chronicles 15:27–29).

Lower City: Home to most of the common people during Jesus' day; built on the slope of the Western Hill, reaching into the Tyropoeon Valley; where Jesus sent the blind man to wash the mud from his eyes in the Pool of Siloam.

Upper City: Highest area in Jerusalem (located on the Western Hill now named Mount Zion), site of Herod's palace, home to wealthy Jews, probably more Hellenists lived here than lived in the Lower City.

Business District: Although not named by ancient sources, this district inside the Second Wall held many shops and markets. The area Jesus walked through on market day on His way to the cross.

New City: During and after Jesus' time, the city expanded north. Many wealthy people lived here. Herod Agrippa walled it about thirty or more years after Jesus' crucifixion.

3. The Sadducees gained wealth and power by controlling the temple's functions. Why do you think they felt so threatened by Jesus? (See John 11:47–48.)

4. Where did Peter go after Jesus was taken prisoner? (See Luke 22:54–56; John 18:12–24.)

5. Think about the differences between the members of the Sanhedrin (John 11:45–53) and Jesus—a poor Galilean rabbi. Why do you think wealth and power were able to corrupt the Sanhedrin?

Topic E: Jesus Takes His Ministry Outside the City Walls

By going through the Garden Gate, people leaving Jerusalem during Jesus' time could reach the area called the New City—the area where the city was expanding to the north. Just outside the gate was an old quarry, where people were taken to be stoned.

1. After the Jewish leaders decided to have Jesus put to death, where was He taken? (See Matthew 27:1–2, 11–31.)

2. Where did the soldiers take Jesus to be crucified? (See Matthew 27:32–33, 39–40; John 19:17–18, 41–42; refer to the map of Jerusalem on page 88.)

3. What routinely happened outside the city walls? What does "going outside the camp" seem to mean? (See Numbers 5:1–4; Hebrews 13:11.)

4. What does it mean to you that Jesus went "outside the city" and faced total rejection in order to die for our sins? (See Leviticus 20:20–22; Hebrews 13:11–12.)

faith Lesson

Time for Reflection

Read the following passage of Scripture silently and take the next few minutes to reflect on God's great work of redemption that took place in the city of Jerusalem and consider what it means to your life.

> Then the governor's soldiers took Jesus into the Praetorium and gathered the whole company of soldiers around him. They stripped him and put a scarlet robe on him, and then twisted together a crown of thorns and set it on his head. They put a staff in his right hand and knelt in front of him and mocked him. "Hail, king of the Jews!" they said. They spit on him, and took the staff and struck him on the head again and again. After they had mocked him, they took off the robe and put his own clothes on him. Then they led him away to crucify him. As they were going out, they met a man from Cyrene, named Simon, and they forced him to carry the cross. They came to a place called Golgotha (which means The Place of the Skull).... Those who passed by hurled insults at him, shaking their heads and saying, "You who are going to destroy the temple and build it in three days, save yourself! Come down from the cross, if you are the Son of God!" In the same way the chief priests, the teachers of the law and the elders mocked him.
>
> MATTHEW 27:27–33, 39–41

1. What do you feel when you realize that Jesus was willing to be your "scapegoat," to go outside the city and symbolically carry your sins into the wilderness in order to enable you to come into His kingdom—His holy city?

2. How will what you've seen and discussed today impact your view of Jerusalem and Jesus?

Action Points

Take a moment to review the key points you explored today. Then write down the action step (or steps) that you will commit to this week as a result of what you have discovered.

1. *To understand more about Jerusalem—its structures, its people, its activity—is to understand the Jewish heritage on which our faith is built.* And as we saw (through the scale model and some actual ruins) what actual structures looked like during Jesus' time—and learned about significant events in His life that took place in or near those structures—the reality of what God did in that city became more real to us.

   Learning about Jewish history and culture—especially Jerusalem—adds greatly to our understanding of Jesus' life and God's redemptive work on earth. The city also gives us a picture of a greater city to come—the heavenly Jerusalem. There, God's faithful will live forever in His presence.

   Until then, His followers are called to bring His love to a broken world, much as God did to Jerusalem throughout history. Just as God initially used the temple to extend His kingdom to the Jews, today God is using us—His temples, His "Jerusalems"—to extend His kingdom throughout the world, to touch the lives of people with God's presence, power, and forgiveness. As His Spirit fills us and lives within us, we are called to take His kingdom to all the people of God's world.

To whom can you take the message of the Messiah during the coming days? Who can you touch with God's presence, power, and forgiveness brought about through Jesus' death and resurrection?

DATA FILE

Where Jerusalem Is Located:

- On a high plateau in the Judea Mountains, about 2,400 feet above sea level. (This location fulfilled Isaiah's prophecy in Isaiah 2:2–3, that people would go up to the mountain of the Lord's house.)
- Thirty miles east of the Mediterranean Sea, twenty miles from the Dead Sea.
- Six miles from Bethlehem where Jesus was born; sixty miles from Nazareth where He grew up; and seventy-five miles from Capernaum where He focused His ministry.

The Lamb of God

Questions to Think About

1. Which words or phrases have you heard people use to describe Jesus?

2. Why do you think people create their own pictures of who Jesus is instead of discovering who the Bible says He is?

3. Which words would *you* use to describe who Jesus is?

video notes

Jesus' Journey Toward Jerusalem

Jesus' Entry into Jerusalem

"Lamb Day"

Passover Politics

Jesus' Tears

video Highlights

Look at the map (on page 106) of the land of Jesus' ministry and note the route Jesus took from Caesarea Philippi to Jerusalem. He stayed on the east side of the Jordan River and traveled through the Decapolis and Peria. Then he crossed the Jordan River north of the Dead Sea at Jericho. From Jericho he went through the Judea Wilderness to Jerusalem.

1. Which aspects of Jesus' entrance into Jerusalem surprised you or were new to you?

2. Imagine that you were in the crowd as Jesus entered Jerusalem. What do you think you'd have felt and thought?

3. In the video, Ray Vander Laan asked us to think about the Jesus who cared so deeply about people that He cried on their behalf. Is this the Jesus you know? Is that a side of Jesus to which you are attracted? Why or why not?

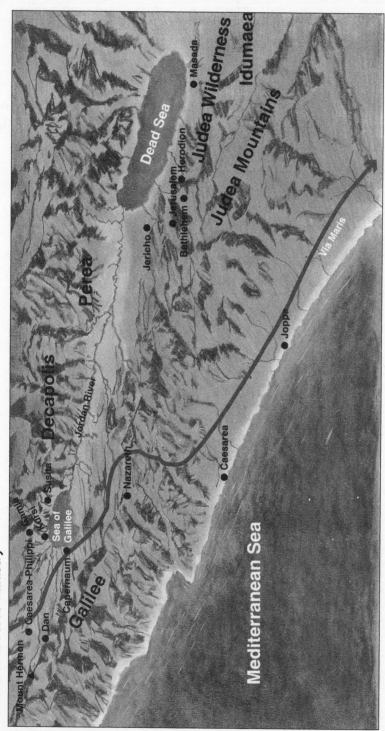

The Land of Jesus' Ministry

small Group Bible Discovery

Topic A: Jesus Presents Himself as the Messiah—the Lamb of God

1. After Peter confessed, on behalf of the disciples, that Jesus was the Messiah (Matthew 16:13–16), Jesus immediately began to teach them about the way in which He would carry out His divine mission. How did the disciples respond to His teaching about His imminent suffering and death? What did their response reveal about their expectations of Jesus? (See Matthew 16:21–25; 17:22–23.)

2. Which principles did Jesus repeatedly seek to communicate to His disciples during this time? (See Matthew 16:24–26; 20:17–27.)

3. What does the Bible say about the disciples' understanding of the kind of Messiah Jesus was? (See John 12:16; Acts 1:4–6.)

4. After walking through the Judea Wilderness, Jesus reached the Mount of Olives and proceeded into Jerusalem, where the people triumphantly acclaimed Him as their king. The following questions will help you to understand the messages Jesus was sending through the manner, timing, and location of His entrance into Jerusalem.

   a. What was the significance of the direction from which Jesus came, in light of Old Testament prophecy? (See Isaiah 40:3.)

   b. Jesus entered the city as Messiah on the tenth day of the month when Jewish families picked Passover lambs for sacrifice. What was He asking the people to recognize? (See Exodus 12:1–6, 12–15; Matthew 17:22–23; John 1:29; John 12:1, 12–18.)

   c. What did Jesus communicate by getting on the donkey as soon as He arrived at Bethphage—the town the rabbis had decided was the city limit of Jerusalem? (See Zechariah 9:9–10; Matthew 21:1–6.)

5. Describe the difference between the way the people responded to Jesus and the way He responded to them (John 12:12–13; Luke 19:38–44).

COMPELLING EVIDENCE

The Messiah from the East

A number of significant events in the history of the Jewish people, particularly events that relate to God's presence, have been recorded as occurring "from the east":

- The children of Israel, with the ark symbolizing God's presence, entered the Promised Land from the east (Joshua 3:1, 15–17).
- In Ezekiel's visions, the glory (presence) of the Lord left the corrupted temple and departed to the east (Ezekiel 10:4, 18–19; 11:22–24).
- Ezekiel also saw the glory of the Lord return to the temple from the east (Ezekiel 43:1–5).
- Jesus' birth was announced in the east (Matthew 2:1–2, 9).
- The prophet Isaiah said that the Messiah would come from the wilderness east of Jerusalem (Isaiah 40:3).
- Jesus ascended into heaven from the Mount of Olives, east of Jerusalem (Acts 1:6–12).
- The Mount of Olives, east of Jerusalem, represents Jesus' Second Coming (Zechariah 14:4; Joel 3:2, 12).

Topic B: Jesus—Our Model for Selfless Sacrifice

1. Look up each of the following verses and consider what Jesus wanted His disciples to be.

   Matthew 5:14

   Matthew 5:43–47

   Matthew 18:1–6

   Matthew 18:21–35

   Matthew 19:13–14

   Matthew 20:20–28

2. Which unusual method did Jesus use to carry out His mission as Messiah? (See Matthew 20:25–28.)

3. In contrast to the example Jesus lived out, what did the disciples want for themselves? (See Matthew 20:20–22.)

4. When Jesus heard what the disciples desired, what did He say to them? (See Matthew 20:25–28.)

FAITH PROFILE

The "Doubting Thomas" Most of Us Never Knew

Most Christians remember Thomas as the disciple who:

- didn't believe the other disciples when they told him they'd seen the risen Jesus (John 20:19–25).
- said that he'd only believe if he touched Jesus' scarred hands and side (John 20:25).

But Thomas was also the disciple who demonstrated great faith and dedication to Jesus during the walk to Jerusalem. When Jesus told His disciples that they were returning to Judea, they protested, recalling that the Jews had tried to stone Him there (John 11:8–9). But Thomas courageously agreed with Jesus, saying, "Let us also go, that we may die with him" (John 11:16). And the disciples remained with Jesus and headed toward Jerusalem.

Topic C: Jesus Turns His Focus on Jerusalem

As Jesus set His course for Jerusalem, He knew He'd face jeering crowds, betrayal by friends, a Roman cross, and finally the rejection of His own Father while He bore the agony of hell for the very people who despised Him. Yet He refused to escape into the Judea Wilderness along the more than ten miles of road from Jericho to Jerusalem.

1. The following verses are in chronological order. Look up each passage and write out what you discover concerning Jesus' goal and His determination to complete His work.

   Matthew 17:22

   Luke 9:51

   Matthew 19:1

   Matthew 20:17–19

   Luke 10:5–7

   Luke 13:22

   Luke 18:31–33

   Matthew 20:29–30

   Matthew 21:1

   Matthew 21:12–16, 23–24

   Matthew 26:1

   Matthew 26:10–12

   Matthew 26:31–32

2. Why was Jesus so determined to go to Jerusalem to die? (See John 12:27–28.)

DATA FILE

The Judea Wilderness

Provided a place to hide:
- David hid from Saul (1 Samuel 23:14).
- Elijah hid from evil Ahab and Jezebel (1 Kings 19:1–5).
- An Egyptian hid from the Roman authorities (Acts 21:8).

Perceived as a place of temptation and evil:
- The name of the scapegoat, who symbolically carried the Israelites' sins into the wilderness, was derived from the Hebrew word *Azazel*. This word apparently came from the name of the goat-demon who was thought to live in the wilderness.
- Goat-gods (satyrs) were believed to live in the wilderness (Leviticus 17:7; 2 Chronicles 11:15; Isaiah 13:21).
- Jewish tradition taught that demons, including a fallen angel, lived there (1 Enoch 6–13).
- Satan tempted Jesus in the wilderness for forty days (Luke 4:1–13).
- Jesus used the wilderness walk between Jerusalem and Jericho as the setting for His parable about the man who was beaten by robbers and left for dead (Luke 10:30–37).

Topic D: Praised as Messiah, But Not as the Lamb of God

1. What did the crowd do as Jesus rode into Jerusalem? (See Matthew 21:6–9; John 12:13.)

2. The word *Hosanna* means "Please save!" (derived from two Hebrew words, *hosha* and *na* found in Psalm 118:25–26). But *save* can mean many different things. What did it mean in the minds of the people?

3. Picture what happened next. The crowd shouted, but Jesus wept! Why did Jesus weep when so many people recognized Him as Messiah? (See Luke 19:41–44.)

4. What is the significance of Jesus coming into Jerusalem on selection day for the Passover lamb? (See John 1:29–36; 1 Corinthians 5:7.)

    a. What is the significance of Jesus choosing to ride the donkey into Jerusalem on lamb selection day? (See Matthew 21:1–7.)

5. Why, as the video has communicated, is it so important for us to recognize Jesus for who He is, not who we want Him to be?

faith Lesson

Time for Reflection

The following Scripture passages reveal the depth of Jesus' love for us. Read these passages silently and consider how greatly Jesus loves you.

The tears of Jesus at Lazarus' tomb:

> On his arrival, Jesus found that Lazarus had already been in the tomb for four days.... When Mary reached the place where Jesus was and saw him, she fell at his feet and said, "Lord, if you had been here, my brother would not have died." When Jesus saw her weeping, and the Jews who had come along with her also weeping, he was deeply moved in spirit and troubled. "Where have you laid him?" he asked. "Come and see, Lord," they replied. Jesus wept. Then the Jews said, "See how he loved him!"
>
> JOHN 11:17, 32–36

The tears of Jesus at Jerusalem:

> After Jesus had said this, he went on ahead, going up to Jerusalem.... When he came near the place where the road goes down the Mount of Olives, the whole crowd of disciples began joyfully to praise God in loud voices for all the miracles they had seen: "Blessed is the king who comes in the name of the Lord!" "Peace in heaven and glory in the highest!" Some of the Pharisees in the crowd said to Jesus, "Teacher, rebuke your disciples!" "I tell you," he replied, "if they keep quiet, the stones will cry out." As he approached Jerusalem and saw the city, he wept over it and said, "If you, even you, had only known on this day what would bring you peace—but now it is hidden from your eyes. The days will come upon you when your enemies will build an embankment against you and encircle you and hem you in on every side. They will dash you to the ground, you and the children within your walls. They will not leave one stone on another, because you did not recognize the time of God's coming to you."
>
> LUKE 19:28, 37–44

1. What was Jesus mourning in each of these instances?

2. What do the tears Jesus shed for the family and friends of Lazarus and the people of Jerusalem reveal about His great love and compassion for people?

3. How does Jesus' determination to travel through the barren wilderness to Jerusalem and die a horrible death for your sins add to your understanding of His great love for you?

4. How has the love of Jesus the Messiah touched your heart and life?

5. How can you help people better understand the loving heart of Jesus the Messiah? How can you help them correctly interpret His message?

Action Points

Take a moment to review the key points you explored today. Then write down an action step (or steps) that you will commit to this week as a result of what you have discovered about Jesus—the Messiah, God's chosen Passover Lamb.

1. *On lamb selection day, Jesus came into Jerusalem as the Lamb of God, but the people—despite their praises—didn't recognize who He was.* He did not fit their idea of what the Messiah would be. They wanted a Messiah who would provide political-military liberation. The vision of a suffering Messiah who would give His life to defeat the "gates of Hades" and to provide freedom from the spiritual bondage of sin was foreign to them. And the idea of following Jesus' example by giving themselves as servants to others was shocking.

   Consequently, many people (including His disciples) did not understand His mission. Most of them wanted political liberation rather than spiritual liberation from sin and the peace of a personal relationship with Him. Because Jesus did not offer what they wanted, many people rejected Him completely.

   In what ways have you misunderstood Jesus and His message?

   In what ways have you reinterpreted Jesus to be what you want Him to be and missed out on what He had to offer?

   What is your commitment to Jesus the Messiah? Will you choose Him as the perfect Lamb of God, the sacrifice for your sins?

2. *Jesus weeps for us. He grieves when we suffer loss and pain, just as He grieved at the tomb of Lazarus.* He also longs for us to recognize and accept Him for who He is. The Messiah who came on "lamb selection day" to establish His kingdom by being a servant and giving up His life as the Lamb of God, wept for the people of Jerusalem when they didn't receive Him as God's Messiah and rejected the deliverance He offered. His heart breaks for us today, just as it did that day in Jerusalem, when we miss Him and His message.

    Why does Jesus weep for you?

The weight of the world

Questions to Think About

1. Which words would you use to describe how you felt during a time when you were under enormous pressure?

2. In contrast, how would you describe what it felt like when that pressure was lifted?

video notes

Symbolism of the Olives

Gethsemane (Olive Press)

The Curse

The Importance of Producing Fruit

video нighlights

1. Which images presented in the video stood out to you? Why?

2. What was Jesus' state of mind that night in Gethsemane? What was the "weight" on Him? Why was He so sorrowful? (See Luke 22:44.)

3. For what did Jesus ask?

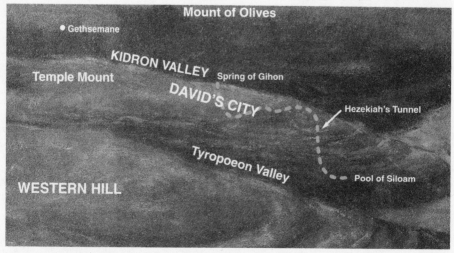

Topography of Jerusalem

Mount of Olives

● Gethsemane

KIDRON VALLEY Spring of Gihon

Temple Mount

DAVID'S CITY

Hezekiah's Tunnel

Tyropoeon Valley

WESTERN HILL

Pool of Siloam

4. Describe the difference between Jesus' mindset and that of His disciples.

5. Why did Jesus curse Capernaum?

6. Why is it important for us to bear fruit in our lives?

small group bible discovery

Topic A: Jesus' Prayer

Look up Matthew 26:39, 42, 44, 47–54; Mark 14:35–36, 39; Luke 22:42.

1. What was Jesus asking in His prayer?

2. What does this prayer reveal about Jesus' relationship with God the Father?

3. What do these verses reveal about God's love for us?

4. Why is it important for us to trust God during difficult times?

5. Which temptations might Jesus have faced during this time?

Topic B: The Disciples' Response

Look up Matthew 26:36–46; Mark 14:37–42; Luke 22:45–46.

1. What did Jesus want the disciples to do? Why do you think He asked that of them?

2. Why do you think the disciples acted so differently from Jesus?

3. Which temptation did the disciples face? How could they have resisted it?

4. If you feel comfortable sharing, describe a time when your friends or family members didn't support you during a crucial time. How did you feel?

5. In what way(s) can you relate to Jesus' loneliness as He faced His anguish alone?

DATA FILE

"Gethsemane"—The word *Gethsemane* is derived from two Hebrew words: *gat*, which means "a place for pressing oil (or wine)" and *she-manim*, which means "oils." During Jesus' time, heavy stone slabs were lowered onto olives that had already been crushed in an olive crusher. Gradually the slabs' weight squeezed the olive oil out of the pulp, and the oil ran into a pit. There the oil was collected in clay jars.

The image of the gethsemane on the slope of the Mount of Olives where Jesus went the night before His crucifixion provides a vivid picture of Jesus' suffering. The weight of the sins of the world pressed down upon Him like a heavy slab of rock pressed down on olives in their baskets. His sweat, "like drops of blood falling to the ground" (Luke 22:44), flowed from Him like olive oil as it was squeezed out and flowed into the pit of an olive press.

Olive Crusher—The stone basin used to crush olives into pulp. A donkey pushed on a horizontal beam, which in turn rolled a millstone that crushed into a pulp ripe olives placed in a large, round basin. An olive crusher was often placed in a cave, where the moderated temperature improved the efficiency of oil production.

An Olive Press

The Amazing Olive Tree

- Its roots can live for more than a thousand years.
- Rarely reaches twenty feet high.
- Must be cut down when it becomes old (often after hundreds of years) in order to become fruitful again. The next year, new shoots will grow out of the stump, and the new olive tree will produce olives again.
- A good olive tree may produce fifty pounds of olives and four to six pounds of oil each year.
- Olive oil was used for food (1 Kings 17:12), skin care (Ecclesiastes 9:7–8), fuel, medicine, and as trade (1 Kings 5:11). It kept leather soft (Isaiah 21:5), priests mixed it with the morning burnt offerings (Exodus 29:40), and it was a symbol of God's Spirit (James 5:14).

Topic C: Christians Are to Bear Fruit

In the Bible, God's relationship to His people is represented by the olive tree, and a Christian's fruitfulness is likened to a tree that bears fruit.

1. In Psalm 52:8, Psalm 128:3, and Hosea 14:5–6, which images are used to describe God's followers?

2. What was the unfaithful nation of Israel compared to? (See Jeremiah 11:16.)

3. What are the consequences of not bearing good fruit? (See Matthew 3:10–12; 7:16–20.)

4. What did God, through Isaiah's prophecy, promise to do with the stump of unfaithful Israel? (See Isaiah 11:1–3; Jeremiah 23:5–6; 33:15–16.)

Topic D: Jesus' Blood Shed for Us

1. What happened to Jesus in Gethsemane as the weight of what He would soon face pressed down on Him? (See Luke 22:40–45.)

2. What do the following verses reveal about the impact of Jesus' shed blood on us today?

Ephesians 1:7

Colossians 1:19–20

Hebrews 13:12

1 John 1:7–10

Revelation 1:4–6

Topic E: Caring for the "Little Ones"
Look up Matthew 18:1–6; Mark 9:33–37, 42.

1. Why do you think Jesus told the disciples to stop thinking of themselves as important?

2. What do you think "becoming like little children" means?

3. Why is humility a less common trait in people today?

4. What did Jesus say would happen to someone who causes a "little one"—someone who seems to be unimportant in society—to stumble in his or her faith?

5. As Ray Vander Laan points out, Jesus felt deeply for the unimportant, for the "little ones" who had no status. Why is it so easy to overlook people in our church . . . school . . . neighborhood . . . who have no status in our world's eyes?

6. Which "little ones" might we tend to overlook today?

7. Which "little ones" are under your leadership or influence right now?

faith Lesson

Time for Reflection

The following Scripture passage describes Jesus' last night in Gethsemane. Read it and take some time to think about the questions that follow it. Consider how you can begin to live out what you have learned through this video.

> Then Jesus went with his disciples to a place called Gethsemane, and he said to them, "Sit here while I go over there and pray." He took Peter and the two sons of Zebedee along with him, and he began to be sorrowful and troubled. Then he said to them, "My soul is overwhelmed with sorrow to the point of death. Stay here and keep watch with me." Going a little farther, he fell with his face to the ground and prayed, "My Father, if it is possible, may this cup be taken from me. Yet not as I will, but as you will." Then he returned to his disciples and found them sleeping. "Could you men not keep watch with me for one hour?" he asked Peter. "Watch and pray so that you will not fall into temptation. The spirit is willing, but the body is weak." He went away a second time and prayed, "My Father, if it is not possible for this cup to be taken away unless I drink it, may your will be done." When he came back he again found them sleeping because their eyes were heavy. So he left them and went away once more and prayed the third time, saying the same thing. Then he returned to the disciples and said to them, "Are you still sleeping and resting? Look, the hour is near, and the Son of Man is betrayed into the hands of sinners. Rise, let us go! Here comes my betrayer!"
>
> MATTHEW 26:36–46

1. Jesus loves each of us with a love we cannot fully compre-
    hend. What did you learn about Jesus' love for you today?
    In what ways can you express your thankfulness to God
    today for what He has done for you?

2. Jesus was willing to pay a terribly high price for our sin.
    Which particular sin in your life right now is hindering
    your walk with Him? Take time to confess your sin to Him
    now and determine to change your ways. If possible, find
    a person to whom you can be accountable in making those
    changes.

3. Why do you think Jesus didn't just disappear into the night
    instead of waiting to be arrested? How would your life be
    different if He had?

4. In which ways might you be a "Capernaum" in that you
    know about Jesus and perhaps have seen Him do special
    things in your life or others' lives, yet have not committed
    your life to Him? What will you do today to reestablish a
    closer relationship with Him?

5. How does the way in which Jesus handled His suffering in Gethsemane relate to the times you face stress, sorrow, and/or agony? What did Jesus do that you can do today during tough times at work? At home? How often do you turn honestly to God in complete devotion to His will?

Action Points

Take a moment to review the key points you explored today. Jot down the action step (or steps) you will take this week.

1. *The olive press—the gethsemane—symbolizes the agonizing weight of our sin that Jesus willingly carried when He was crucified.* Our sins are like the big rock in the olive press that forced the olive oil out of the olives. We were the burden He bore. Our guilt and the required penalty for sin were great, but Jesus' love for us and His obedient devotion to His Father's will were greater. Despite the powerful emotions He felt, Jesus submitted completely to His Father's will.

    > "He was pierced for our transgressions, he was crushed for our iniquities; the punishment that brought us peace was upon him, and by his wounds we are healed." (Isaiah 53:5)

    > "He himself bore our sins in his body on the tree, so that we might die to sins and live for righteousness; by his wounds you have been healed." (1 Peter 2:24)

    Recognizing the weight that Jesus bore, how will you view your sins differently this week?

2. *You must choose how you will respond to what Jesus has done for you.* Because of His deep love and compassion, Jesus willingly accepted the agonizing burden of our sin and went to the cross alone. He willingly died for our sins—a miracle that only He could perform. You can respond with thanksgiving and dedicate your life to following Him, or you can fail to respond to what Jesus has done for you.

How will you respond this week to the love Jesus demonstrated for you?

3. *How you respond to what Jesus has done for you has serious consequences.* If you know what Jesus has done for you and understand His words, yet do not respond positively to Him and what He has done for you, you will be judged accordingly.

Jesus cursed the people in His hometown of Capernaum, saying, "If the miracles that were performed in you had

JESUS: OUR SOURCE OF LIFE

When an olive tree that is being cared for becomes too old, it stops bearing fruit and is cut down. From the stump, a new branch is cultivated into a new olive tree. Thousands of years before Jesus came to earth, the prophet Isaiah compared Jesus—the Messiah (the "anointed one")—to a new shoot that will spring out of the unbelieving nation of Israel and revitalize it. When we become Christians, we are in a sense grafted into Jesus—our life-giving branch. We gain our life and energy from Him.

been performed in Sodom, it would have remained to this day. But I tell you that it will be more bearable for Sodom on the day of judgment than for you" (Matthew 11:23–24). They saw Jesus' love in action and knew what to do, yet didn't respond positively to Him and chose to do evil.

But if you submit completely to Jesus and allow God to live through you, you will be spiritually fruitful and derive your life from Him.

What kind of fruit will you produce this week? Will you yield yourself to Jesus daily, or will you be unresponsive to His will for your life?

Roll Away the Stone

Questions to Think About

1. In what ways has the resurrection of Jesus changed the course of human history?

2. What hope does the resurrection provide for all of humanity?

3. How would your faith and life be different if Jesus had not been raised from the dead?

video notes

Blowing of the Shofar

The Gift of the Tomb

The Stone Rolled Away

The Offering of the Cup

video нighlights

1. What insights into Jesus' sacrificial death, burial, and resurrection did you gain by watching this video?

2. Why was the gift of the tomb so remarkable?

3. In what ways might you view the death and resurrection of Jesus as "the defining event in the New Testament"?

4. What did the stone being rolled away from the door of the tomb enable Jesus' disciples to do? Why was this important then? Why is it important today?

Jerusalem's Districts

A David's City
B New City
C Upper City
D Business District
E Temple Mount
F Lower City
G Herod's Palace

1 Eastern Gate
2 Southern Stairs
3 Royal Stoa
4 Robinson's Arch
5 Wilson's Arch
6 Tyropoeon Street
7 Warren's Gate
8 Antonia
9 Tadi Gate
10 Pool of Bethesda
11 First Wall
12 Second Wall
13 Garden Gate
14 Towers (Damascus) Gate
15 Golgotha (?)
16 Garden Tomb
17 Spring of Gihon
18 Hinnom Valley
19 Theater
20 Citadel and Herod's Palace
21 Essene Quarter
22 Mansions
23 Mount of Olives
24 Kidron Valley
25 Huldah Gates

5. What price did Jesus pay in order to offer the cup of salvation to you and me?

6. How does Jesus want us to respond to His offer of salvation?

A typical first-century family tomb

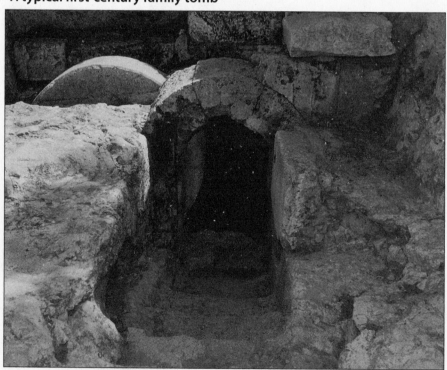

small group bible discovery

Topic A: Jesus' Crucifixion Prophesied

Compare the actual events surrounding Jesus' crucifixion with the Old Testament prophesies. Record your answers in the chart below:

1. What did the soldiers do to Jesus? (See Psalm 22:16–18; John 19:23–24; Mark 15:25–32.)

2. What exception was made in Jesus' case? (See Psalm 34:20; John 19:32–34; Zechariah 12:10.)

3. What was Jesus given to drink while on the cross? (See Psalm 69:21; Matthew 27:48.)

4. What did Isaiah predict would happen to Jesus? (See Isaiah 53:3.)

Old Testament Prophecy	Did it happen?
1.	
2.	
3.	
4.	

5. Who rejected Jesus, as recorded in each of the following passages?

John 6:66

John 7:47–53

Matthew 26:14–16

Matthew 26:56

Matthew 26:69–75

Matthew 27:46

Topic B: Jesus' Sacrifice for Our Sin—He Died as God's Lamb

1. Under which circumstances did the first Passover take place? (See Exodus 12:1–7, 12–14.)

2. When were subsequent Passovers to be celebrated? (See Leviticus 23:5.)

3. What is the significance of what John the Baptist said about Jesus early in His ministry? (See John 1:29.)

4. Which words did Paul use to describe Jesus? (See 1 Corinthians 5:7b.)

5. In Hebrews 9:11–15, what do we learn about the importance of Christ's blood?

6. What does the timing of Jesus' death say about God's planning? (See Luke 23:44.)

JESUS, THE LAMB OF THE WORLD

During Old Testament times, perhaps even going back to the time of Moses, the Jewish priests traditionally slaughtered the Passover sacrifice at 3:00 in the afternoon after blowing a shofar—a special horn. They then offered the sacrifice at 3:30, following the daily sacrifice. Both the daily sacrifice and the Passover sacrifice were offered to symbolically cleanse the nation of Israel of its sin.

At exactly 3:00 (the "ninth hour" as the Bible puts it in Luke 23:45), just as the Passover lamb was being killed, Jesus looked up into heaven and said, "Father, into your hands I commit my spirit."

Topic C: The Empty Tomb

Look up Matthew 27:62–65; 28:1–10; Luke 24:9–12.

1. When the earthquake occurred, and the angel appeared, and the stone was rolled away, what happened to the Roman guards?

2. How did the women respond when they saw the empty tomb and the angel? When they realized the truth of what had happened?

WHAT WAS THE TOMB REALLY LIKE?

- It belonged to a rich Jewish man named Joseph of Arimathea (Matthew 27:57–60), who was a prominent member of the Jewish Council (Mark 15:43).
- It had never been used before. According to Jewish law held by the Pharisees, only people in an immediate family could be buried in the same tomb, so it is likely that no one in the family of Joseph of Arimathea would ever use it again.
- It was cut from rock and sealed with a large stone (Matthew 27:59–60; Mark 16:4). Often the stone for this type of tomb weighed more than two tons and was rolled across the opening of the tomb.
- It was brand new (Luke 23:50–53).
- It had a low door and was large enough to hold more than one person (Luke 24:1–4, 12; Mark 16:1–5).
- It was located near a garden (John 19:38–42).
- People could see into it without entering it (John 20:1–8).

3. How did the disciples respond when they heard the news?

4. Why was it necessary for Jesus' followers to see the empty tomb?

5. What difference should the empty tomb make in our lives today?

Topic D: Committing Ourselves to Jesus

As explained in the video, a man and woman in Jesus' day sealed their engagement by exchanging a cup of wine. The bride accepted the cup from her future husband as an indication of her lifelong commitment to him.

1. To whom did Jesus compare Himself? (See Mark 2:18–19.)

2. In light of what you learned in the video, what was the significance of Jesus offering the third cup of salvation to His disciples during the Passover celebration in the Upper Room? (See Luke 22:20.)

DATA FILE

The Symbolism of the Cup

The Marriage Cup. During biblical times, a young man who wanted to marry would accompany his father to the chosen woman's house, where she and her father would be present. They'd negotiate a steep "bride price"—the money or physical items that the woman's father would ask for in exchange for giving up his valuable daughter.

Then the young man's father would hand his son a cup of wine. The son, in turn, would offer it to the woman and say, "This cup I offer to you." In effect he was saying, "I love you, and I offer you my life. Will you marry me?" If she drank it (sealing their engagement), she accepted his life and gave him hers. If not, she simply declined.

The Passover Cup. During the Passover liturgy of Jesus' day, participants would drink from four cups of wine at different times. The third cup was called the cup of salvation. While celebrating the Passover with His disciples in the Upper Room, Jesus offered them the cup of salvation and said, "This cup is a new covenant in My blood." He was saying, in effect, "I love you. I give you My life. Will you marry Me? Will you be My spiritual bride? Will you give your life to Me?"

So, every time we drink from the Communion cup when the minister says, "This cup is a new covenant in my blood," God is saying to us, "I love you. I invite you to be My spiritual bride." And every time we drink it, we are in effect saying to Him, "I accept Your gift, and I give You my life in return."

The Cup from Which Jesus Drank in Order to Become Our Spiritual Husband. Jesus asked His Father the night before He died, "If it is possible, may this cup be taken from me" (Matthew 26:39). He knew the high price He would have to pay to purchase His bride and become our spiritual husband.

3. In Revelation 19:6–8, what do the "Lamb" and "his bride" symbolize?

4. In light of the symbolism of the cup, what are we, in effect, saying to God when we drink the cup during Communion? How do you live out that commitment in your daily life?

Topic E: The Torn Curtain in the Temple

1. Where did God make His presence known to the people of Israel? (See Leviticus 16:2; Hebrews 9:1–4.)

2. Who was the only person who could enter the inner room behind the curtain? (See Hebrews 9:7.)

3. Why did the high priest offer a blood offering? (See Hebrews 9:7–9.)

COMPELLING EVIDENCE

There is an abundance of evidence in Scripture and in the religious practices of the Jews that God carefully planned the timing of Jesus' death and resurrection. The following are just a few examples of God's planning:

- Prophecies given hundreds of years before Jesus was even born were precisely fulfilled when Jesus died.
- The high priest's practice of killing the Passover Lamb had been in force for hundreds, perhaps a thousand, years. On Friday of the year Jesus died, the Jews celebrated Passover and killed a lamb for the temple sacrifice. Jesus, the Lamb of God, died at that same time in order to take our sins upon Himself.
- The year that Jesus died, Saturday—the Sabbath—was also the day on which the Jews celebrated the Feast of Unleavened Bread. This feast reminded the Jews of the bread that God provided for the Israelites when they left Egypt. Consider the significant parallels between this feast and Jesus' death:

Wheat seeds must die in order to bring forth their crop.	Jesus had to die and be buried in order to accomplish His ministry and be raised to new life.
Unleavened bread was made without yeast, because yeast represented sin (1 Corinthians 5:7–8).	Jesus, the Lamb of God, was sinless.

- On the Sunday following Jesus' death, the Israelites celebrated the Feast of Firstfruits, which in this case celebrated the beginning of the barley harvest. The Israelites returned to God the "first part" of everything they had been given to indicate: their thankfulness for the harvest; their acknowledgment that God had given them the gifts; and their faith that God would continue to provide (Numbers 15:17–21; Deuteronomy 26:1–11). They gave the best first part of what they received to God (Exodus 23:19). Also, on that day Jesus came to life as God's Firstfruits—the guarantee that the rest would follow—including the resurrection of the dead (1 Corinthians 15:20–23).

4. What did Jesus' death accomplish through the shedding of His blood? (See Hebrews 9:12.)

5. What did Jesus—the unblemished Lamb of God—do to make the temple curtain obsolete? (See Matthew 27:50–51; Hebrews 9:14.)

6. How did Jesus' death and resurrection affect our access to the very presence of God?

faith Lesson

Time for Reflection

The following Scripture passage describes the responses of some of Jesus' followers to His death and resurrection. Read this passage silently and consider your own response to God's great work of salvation.

As evening approached, there came a rich man from Arimathea, named Joseph, who had himself become a disciple of Jesus. Going to Pilate, he asked for Jesus' body, and Pilate ordered that it be given to him. Joseph took the body, wrapped it in a clean linen cloth, and placed it in his own new tomb that he had cut out of the rock. He rolled a big stone in front of the entrance to the tomb and went away. Mary Magdalene and the other Mary were sitting there opposite the tomb.

MATTHEW 27:57–61

After the Sabbath, at dawn on the first day of the week, Mary Magdalene and the other Mary went to look at the tomb. There was a violent earthquake, for an angel of the Lord came down from heaven and, going to the tomb, rolled back the stone and sat on it. His appearance was like lightning, and his clothes were white as snow. The guards were so afraid of him that they shook and became like dead men. The angel said to the women, "Do not be afraid, for I know that you are looking for Jesus, who was crucified. He is not here; he has risen, just as he said. Come and see the place where he lay. Then go quickly and tell his disciples: 'He has risen from the dead and is going ahead of you into Galilee. There you will see him.' Now I have told you." So the women hurried away from the tomb, afraid yet filled with joy, and ran to tell his disciples. Suddenly Jesus met them. "Greetings," he said. They came to him, clasped his feet and worshiped him. Then Jesus said to them, "Do not be afraid. Go and tell my brothers to go to Galilee; there they will see me."

MATTHEW 28:1–10

1. When Joseph of Arimathea—a public figure—asked for Jesus' body and willingly placed it in his costly new tomb, he made a great sacrifice that expressed deep devotion. In what way could you demonstrate a similar level of sacrificial devotion to Jesus?

2. When Joseph of Arimathea boldly asked Pilate for Jesus' body, his expression of love for Jesus went against the tide of the other members of the Jewish council. Have you ever spoken out for Jesus in a setting where your views were unpopular? In what ways are you willing to stand against the tide—of your friends? Of your family? Of the culture in which you live?

3. If you could go back in time and see the empty tomb of Jesus, how might you live your life differently? What does your answer reveal about your faith?

4. What effect does the reality of Jesus' resurrection have on your life today? In what specific ways do you live differently because Jesus is alive today?

Action Points

Take a moment to review the key points you explored today. Then write down an action step (or steps) that you will commit to this week as a result of what you have discovered.

1. *Jesus made the ultimate sacrifice for us by offering up His sinless life.* He has offered us the cup of salvation—His marriage cup, His life. He invites us to accept the cup of salvation. It is up to us to choose whether or not we will drink from it and thereby accept His gift and commit our lives to Him each day.

   In what ways has Jesus proven His love to you? What must you do this week to faithfully live out your commitment to Him?

2. *Jesus' resurrection proclaimed God's power over everything—Roman soldiers, the cross, even physical death.* But it's not enough to know that Jesus was buried. We must, symbolically, look into the tomb for ourselves and say, "I know Jesus is alive!" We must believe that and live accordingly.

   Are you living as if Jesus were still in the tomb? How might you tap into the power of God that raised Jesus from the dead and live more fully as a child of the risen Lord?

3. *Just as the angel rolled away the stone in front of the tomb so that Jesus' disciples could see that He had risen, we must, in effect, be instruments of God and roll the stone away so that other people can see that the tomb is empty, too!*

Which person has God brought into your life who needs to meet the resurrected Christ? How might God want you to respond to him or her this week?

In light of the fact that Jesus sacrificed His life for me, in light of the fact that the stone has been rolled away, I will:

As you make this commitment, meditate on the great work God accomplished for you through Jesus' death and resurrection as expressed in the words of the closing song of the video.

> *How beautiful the hands that served,*
> *The wine and the bread and the sons of the earth.*
> *How beautiful the feet that walked,*
> *The long dusty road and the hill to the cross.*
> *How beautiful the heart that bled,*
> *That took all my sin and bore it instead.*
> *And as he lay down his life,*
> *We offer this sacrifice,*
> *That we should give, live just as he died.*
> *Willing to pay the price.*
> *Willing to pay the price.*
> *How beautiful the radiant bride,*
> *Who waits for her groom with his light in her eyes.*
> *How beautiful, how beautiful, how beautiful,*
> *Is the body of Christ.*

power to the people

questions to think about

1. Think about a time when you faced what seemed like an insurmountable challenge. What or who gave you the courage and willpower to keep going?

2. How would you describe a *Pentecost* Christian? What is the evidence of the Holy Spirit within that person?

video notes

The Southern Stairs on Pentecost (Shavuot) Morning

The Disciples After Jesus' Ascension

Evidence of God's Indwelling Presence

video нighlights

1. What impact does the possibility that the "house" in which the disciples gathered on Pentecost morning was the temple have on your understanding of God's work at Pentecost?

2. How do you think the disciples felt when they found themselves filled with the Holy Spirit and realized that God's power—the power they had seen Jesus demonstrate time and again—was within them?

3. What did God command the celebrants of the Feast of Pentecost to do in order to express their thanksgiving?

4. What immediately happened after the disciples received the Holy Spirit?

small group bible discovery

Topic A: Remembering God's Faithfulness During Difficult Times

1. Immediately after Jesus' crucifixion, what was the mood of the disciples? What happened to their faith? (See Luke 24:1–4, 9–22; Mark 16:8–14; Luke 24:36–37; John 20:19.)

2. How did the disciples' mood change after Jesus' resurrection? (See Matthew 28:8–10, 16–17; Luke 24:36–42; John 20:19–20.)

3. What was the disciples' mood after Jesus' ascension? What happened to their faith? (See Luke 24:50–53.)

4. Why did the disciples' mood improve after Jesus' ascension?

5. Which truths and principles from the disciples' experience can we cling to today when we face seemingly impossible difficulties, when we feel as if God has abandoned us, or when we don't know which way to turn?

Topic B: When the Church Was Born

On the map of the city of Jerusalem locate the temple and the Southern Stairs. Imagine the whole city filled with visitors and thousands upon thousands of worshippers going into the temple on Pentecost morning.

1. After Jesus ascended to heaven, what did the disciples do? What does their activity reveal about them? (See Luke 24:50–53.)

2. After the Holy Spirit came upon Jesus' disciples, why were the nearby Jews who had come from many lands bewildered? (See Acts 2:5–12.)

3. What was the result of Peter's preaching? (See Acts 2:37–41.)

Jerusalem's Districts

A   David's City
B   New City
C   Upper City
D   Business District
E   Temple Mount
F   Lower City
G   Herod's Palace
1   Eastern Gate
2   Southern Stairs
3   Royal Stoa
4   Robinson's Arch
5   Wilson's Arch
6   Tyropoeon Street
7   Warren's Gate
8   Antonia
9   Tadi Gate
10 Pool of Bethesda
11 First Wall
12 Second Wall
13 Garden Gate
14 Towers (Damascus) Gate
15 Golgotha (?)
16 Garden Tomb
17 Spring of Gihon
18 Hinnom Valley
19 Theater
20 Citadel and Herod's Palace
21 Essene Quarter
22 Mansions
23 Mount of Olives
24 Kidron Valley
25 Huldah Gates

4. What continued to occur in the young church during the days immediately following Pentecost? (See Acts 4:4; 5:14; 6:7.)

5. Why were the Jews scattered throughout the world at this period in time? (See 2 Kings 17:23; 2 Chronicles 36:20.)

6. Why was it important in God's plan that Jews from every nation become followers of Jesus?

7. In what way did the events of Pentecost fulfill Shavuot? (See Matthew 9:37–38; Luke 10:1–3; John 4:34–38.)

Topic C: The Physical Evidence of God's Spirit

God's presence had been physically evident prior to the birth of the church at Pentecost. Let's take a closer look at several significant manifestations of God's Spirit that occurred at the giving of the law, the setting up of the tabernacle, and the dedication of the temple.

1. In what ways was the Spirit of God evident when Moses was on Mount Sinai? (See Exodus 19:16–19.)

COMPELLING EVIDENCE

Consider the similarities in the manifestations of God's presence on Mount Sinai and during Pentecost. Is it simply a coincidence?

On Mount Sinai	During Pentecost
God's presence was accompanied by fire, smoke, and the sound of thunder (Exodus 19:16–19).	God's presence was accompanied by the sound of wind, tongues of fire, and the gift of languages (Acts 2:1–3). The Hebrew term translated "Holy Spirit," *Ruach HaKodesh*, means "Holy Wind."
When God gave the Torah to Moses, the people were worshiping the golden calf. About 3,000 people died as punishment for their sins (Exodus 32:1–4, 19–20, 27–28).	When Jesus' Spirit was given, the people repented, and about 3,000 people believed and found spiritual life (Acts 2:41).
The Law was written on stone tablets (Exodus 31:18).	The Law was written on the hearts of the people (2 Corinthians 3:3; Jeremiah 31:33).
God's presence was symbolized by a cloud and fire, which had led the Israelites out of Egypt. Later, God moved His presence into the temple (2 Chronicles 5:7–8, 13–14).	God's presence moved from the temple into a "new temple"—the followers of Jesus (Romans 8:9; 1 Corinthians 3:16–17).
The Torah (*Torah* means "teaching") provided God's teachings for the Old Testament community of people.	The Holy Spirit became the Teacher of believers (John 14:26).
God met Moses—the Israelites' leader—on Mount Sinai, "the mountain of God" (Exodus 24:13).	Jerusalem was built on a mountain called "the mountain of the Lord" (Isaiah 2:3; 66:20).

2. How did God make His presence known in the Tent of
    Meeting, or tabernacle, during the Israelites' travels to the
    Promised Land? (See Exodus 40:34–38.)

3. At the dedication of Solomon's temple, how did the
    Israelites know that God had taken up residence there?
    2 Chronicles 5:7, 11–14:

    2 Chronicles 7:1–3:

    2 Chronicles 7:11–12, 15–16:

4. Describe what it was like when the Holy Spirit moved from
    the temple building into a new temple—that of Jesus' dis-
    ciples. (See Acts 2:1–5.)

Topic D: The History of the Feast of Weeks (Pentecost)

1. When, as God spoke through Moses, was the Feast of
    Weeks (Pentecost) to take place? (See Leviticus 23:15–22;
    Deuteronomy 16:9–12.)

2. The Feast of Weeks was celebrated during the month
    Sivan—the third month. Which other significant event
    occurred during the third month? (See Exodus 19:1).

3. What were celebrants to present to God during the Feast of Weeks—the feast in honor of the end of the wheat harvest? (See Leviticus 23:16–22; Numbers 28:26–31.)

4. Who was required to attend Pentecost—and the other two feasts—and appear before God in the temple? (See Deuteronomy 16:16.)

5. List the subjects of the Scriptures that were read in the synagogue and temple on Pentecost:

Scripture Reading	Subject
Exodus 19:1–20:26	
Ezekiel 1:22–28	
The Book of Ruth	

6. What insights do these readings provide concerning the events of the Christian Pentecost?

Topic E: A Call to Action—The Evidence of Pentecost

1. In addition to bringing offerings to the temple, how were the celebrants of the Feast of Weeks (Pentecost) to demonstrate their thankfulness? (See Leviticus 19:9–10; 23:22.)

DATA FILE

Pentecost—The History of the Feast

The Feast of Weeks (also called *Shavuot,* in Hebrew; *Pentecoste,* by Greek-speaking Jews; and "the day of firstfruits") celebrated the end of the wheat harvest. It was a time to bring thank offerings to God and, according to Jewish tradition, the time when God gave Moses the Torah on Mount Sinai.

- Instituted by God more than 1,200 years before Jesus sent His Spirit to indwell the disciples, the Feast of Weeks was one of three feasts during which all Jewish men were required to appear before God in the temple (Deuteronomy 16:16).
- The Feast of Weeks was celebrated fifty days after Passover Sabbath (Leviticus 23:16). Because of this, it was called *Pentecost,* a word derived from the Greek word translated "fifty days" (Acts 2:1).
- People who celebrated Pentecost were to show concern for the poor by not harvesting the edges of their fields and leaving the grain they dropped during the harvest for those in need to gather (Leviticus 19:9–10; 23:22).

Pentecost—The Birthplace of the Church

For Christians, Pentecost is considered to be the day when the Holy Spirit left the temple and came in visible, audible form and miraculously filled the disciples with God's power. It is the day on which the Christian church—the community of believers—was born.

Although it is commonly believed that the disciples were in the Upper Room when they were filled with the Holy Spirit, that is unlikely. Here's why:

- Crowds of people were present (Acts 2:5–6). These people would not have fit into a small room. Clearly masses of people would have been in the temple on Pentecost.
- The disciples were continually in the temple (Luke 24:53) and would have been there during the day of Pentecost.

- Pentecost was one of the holiest days of the year, and it is likely that they were in the temple for worship and to hear the readings at 9:00 A.M. (Acts 2:15).
- The disciples were in "the house" (Acts 2:1–2) when the Holy Spirit came upon them. Many Old Testament passages referred to the temple as "the house." However, the English translation is rendered "temple." (See Ezekiel 40:5, 42:15, and 43:10 in the King James Version.)
- Peter described his location as being near the tomb of David (Acts 2:29). According to 1 Kings 2:10, David was buried in the "City of David"—the part of Jerusalem near the Temple Mount.

So where were the disciples? No one knows for sure, but they were in the vicinity of the temple, perhaps in the temple courts or on the Southern Stairs where thousands of Jewish pilgrims would have gathered. Consider the evidence:

- The Southern Stairs led from the valley below, where David's City was located, to the double gates by the main processional entrance to the temple. Many thousands of pilgrims at a time walked up the Southern Stairs to the huge temple platform (about 900 by 1,500 feet) that surrounded the marble temple.
- The Southern Stairs were also known as the "Rabbi's Teaching Staircase" because they were a prime location for rabbis to teach their disciples. (Some scholars believe that Jesus' final discourse on the end of the world, found in Luke 21, took place as He left the temple by the Southern Stairs.) Listeners could sit on the broad, stone steps, and passersby could gather and listen, too.
- Nearby ceremonial baths would have made it convenient for the disciples to baptize the approximately 3,000 people who became believers after the Holy Spirit came upon the disciples. These baths were one of the few places where there would have been sufficient water to baptize that many people.

2. When the early Christians were filled with the Holy Spirit, how did they respond to one another and to the needs of other people? (See Acts 2:44–47.)

3. What is the fruit of the Spirit? (See Galatians 5:22–26.)

4. In what ways does this list relate to the fulfillment of Pentecost?

PENTECOST PROFILE:

Boaz—His Love for One Needy Person Changed the World

Each year on Pentecost, the Jews read the Old Testament book of Ruth. It tells the story of an Israelite couple who moved to Moab during a famine in Canaan. The husband and two sons died, leaving the mother (Naomi) and her two daughters-in-law alone. Naomi chose to return to Israel, and one of her daughters-in-law, Ruth, insisted on accompanying her.

Naomi had a relative on her husband's side named Boaz, and Ruth began picking up the barley left in his fields after harvest. Boaz had compassion on the destitute Gentile woman and provided generously for her. Eventually he recognized his God-given responsibility and married her.

Little did Boaz know how the help he provided changed the world! Ruth had a son, who became the father of Jesse, who was the father of David—the lineage from which Jesus came! (See Matthew 1—the genealogy of Jesus.)

By helping just one needy person in Jesus' name, you could truly make an eternal impact.

faith Lesson

Time for Reflection

The following passages of Scripture reveal the work of the Holy Spirit in the lives of early believers. Read these passages silently and consider the significance of what happened on Pentecost and how the indwelling Spirit of God affects your life.

But you will receive power when the Holy Spirit comes on you; and you will be my witnesses in Jerusalem, and in all Judea and Samaria, and to the ends of the earth.

ACTS 1:8

All of them were filled with the Holy Spirit and began to speak in other tongues as the Spirit enabled them. Now there were staying in Jerusalem God-fearing Jews from every nation under heaven. When they heard this sound, a crowd came together in bewilderment, because each one heard them speaking in his own language. Utterly amazed, they asked: "Are not all these men who are speaking Galileans? Then how is it that each of us hears them in his own native language?" ... Amazed and perplexed, they asked one another, "What does this mean?"

ACTS 2:4–8, 12

"Therefore let all Israel be assured of this: God has made this Jesus, whom you crucified, both Lord and Christ." When the people heard this, they were cut to the heart and said to Peter and the other apostles, "Brothers, what shall we do?" Peter replied, "Repent and be baptized, every one of you, in the name of Jesus Christ for the forgiveness of your sins. And you will receive the gift of the Holy Spirit. The promise is for you and your children and for all who are far off— for all whom the Lord our God will call." With many other words he warned them; and he pleaded with them, "Save yourselves from this corrupt generation." Those who accepted his message were baptized, and about three thousand were added to their number that day.

ACTS 2:36–41

All the believers were one in heart and mind. No one claimed that any of his possessions was his own, but they shared everything they had. With great power the apostles continued to testify to the resurrection of the Lord Jesus, and much grace was upon them all.

ACTS 4:32–33

1. As Christians, we are to be to our world what the temple was to the world of the Old Testament. We are to reflect God's indwelling presence. Think about what this meant— in terms of practical, day-to-day living—for the early Christians and what it produced in their lives.

    a. What does it mean for you to reflect God's presence to your world?

    b. What might be the result?

    c. Think about what it means to be a *Pentecost* Christian. What evidence of the Spirit's presence can be seen in your desire to help other people in need?

A PENTECOST CHRISTIAN:
• Asks God to indwell him or her in order to reflect God's presence to the world.
• Brings a spiritual harvest to God by testifying of Him to other people.
• Demonstrates the presence of God's Spirit by caring for people in need.

2. At Pentecost, God empowered His disciples to be His witnesses, and with great power they testified to the resurrection of the Lord Jesus.

a. What has God empowered you to do?

b. Are you trusting Him to lead you to accomplish His purposes through you?

c. How might you seek out God's Spirit and become a more powerful witness to your needy world?

Action Points

If we have God's Spirit, God calls us to be His witnesses and to bring in the spiritual harvest. Empowered by His Holy Spirit, we are to share Him with other people so that they, too, can develop a personal relationship with Him and reflect Him to the world. Take a moment to highlight the key points you have explored today. Then write down the step (or steps) of commitment or action that you are willing to make as a result of what you have discovered.

1. *God has called and empowered His people—the church—to be His witnesses.* On Pentecost, God gave His power to His people so that they might be His witnesses "in Jerusalem, and in all Judea and Samaria, and to the ends of the earth" (Acts 1:8).

   In what ways can you be a more powerful witness for God in your world? At home? At work? In your neighborhood?

2. *Christians are God's temple.* The Holy Spirit worked a great miracle on the day of Pentecost. The presence of God entered a new "temple"—the community of believers. His Spirit has filled this new temple and empowers us to do what He calls us to do.

   What are you willing to do in order to obediently and courageously reflect God's presence and impact a world that desperately needs Him?

3. *The reality of Pentecost is made evident by the way in which we care for other people.* Pentecost was a holiday of thanksgiving to God. In addition to worshiping in the temple, the

people demonstrated their thanksgiving by caring for needy people. When God fulfilled Pentecost by sending His Holy Spirit upon the disciples, the early Christians immediately began meeting one another's needs. When you and I are filled with God's Spirit, our response will be to willingly and gratefully share our resources and our lives with people in need.

Whose needs will you seek to meet this week? This month? This year?

What will you share with those individuals?

Total commitment

Questions to Think About

1. What do people today pursue in order to appear success-
   ful? What kinds of monuments to themselves do they
   build?

2. What are some of the false truths that motivate people to
   spend lots of money, time, and energy to promote themselves and/or to build monuments to themselves?

3. What kind of legacy do you want to leave? What would
   you like other people to say about you after you die? Be
   specific. Write down your answer.

video notes

The Wonders of Caesarea

Caesarea: The Gospel's Gateway to the Gentile World

The Stones Symbolizing Herod and David

video Highlights

1. What was so remarkable about Caesarea during Herod's time?

2. What were your thoughts about the way people today (including yourself) live as you discovered what Herod lived for and then saw the ruins of his great city?

3. Which truths stood out to you as Ray Vander Laan compared the two stones—the marble fragment and the ordinary sling stone—to Herod and David?

DATA FILE

The Glory of Caesarea

A Theater
B Palace
C Temple of Augustus
D Harbor (Sebastos)
E Lighthouse
F Aqueduct
G Amphitheater
H Hippodrome

The Harbor

- No natural harbor existed, so Herod constructed a harbor using two breakwaters. The south breakwater was 600 yards (1800 feet) long, the north breakwater was 300 yards long.
- The base for these breakwaters was built of 40-foot by 50-foot concrete blocks that were poured under water at depths up to 100 feet.
- The towering lighthouse at the harbor entrance could be seen for miles.
- Harbor facilities included vaulted storage rooms along the breakwaters.

The Remains of the Pool in the Palace at Caesarea

The Palace

- Located on its own peninsula, the palace included a small port so that Herod's visitors could enter the palace without stepping into the city.
- Its pool—115 feet long, 60 feet wide, and 8 feet deep—extended into the salty Mediterranean Sea, yet it most likely held fresh water.
- Herod welcomed his guests with luxurious rooms that included a large dining hall, hot and cold baths, and a semicircular colonnade that extended out into the sea.
- Most likely, Paul was held prisoner here for at least two years before he departed for Rome to appeal to the emperor.

The Theater

- It was located outside the city, probably because the bawdy and obscene performances that took place there were so offensive to Jewish residents.
- It was an important tool in promoting Hellenism—a people-centered lifestyle that glorified human knowledge, accomplishment, and experience.

- Positioned so that prevailing breezes provided amazingly good acoustics, the theater could hold about 4,000 spectators, who sat on stone benches.
- It may have been the site where Paul presented his magnificent defense of the gospel to Felix, Festus, Agrippa II, and Bernice.

The Temple of Augustus

- Dedicated to the goddess Roma and the "divine" emperor Augustus, it was one of the largest temples in the world at that time.
- Built on a great platform, the temple itself towered an additional 100 feet.
- It was coated with plaster made from marble dust, which made it gleam white in the sun.

The Hippodrome and Amphitheater

- It is not yet known if Herod actually built these facilities, but it is known that he promoted Hellenism by sponsoring sports festivals such as those that would take place in such facilities.
- The games that took place in these facilities were dedicated to pagan gods, were performed in the nude, at times involved human bloodshed, and were considered by religious Jews to be immoral.

The Aqueduct

- Since there was no fresh-water source in Caesarea, it provided the city and Herod's palace with water from springs on the slopes of Mount Carmel.
- It extended nearly nine miles from the city to the base of Mount Carmel, plus had an additional six miles of shafts and tunnels that burrowed into the mountain itself.
- It was an amazing engineering feat. It carried water in a plastered channel (much of which rested on a series of arches) across a river and through a channel cut into the sandstone hills.

small Group Bible Discovery

Topic A: Caesarea — Where Gentiles First Received God's Spirit

1. Who was Cornelius? Where did he live? What do we know about his lifestyle? (See Acts 10:1–2.)

2. Which unusual spiritual events happened to Cornelius and to Peter? (See Acts 10:3–16.)

3. After Cornelius's messengers found Peter, what unusual thing did Peter do? (See Acts 10:23–33.)

4. What happened as Peter shared the message of Jesus with the Gentiles in Caesarea? What was the response of the Jews who were with Peter? (See Acts 10:44–48.)

Topic B: The Herods—A Legacy of Rejection

1. How did Herod Agrippa, grandson of Herod the Great who built Caesarea, respond to the message of Jesus being spread throughout his realm? (See Acts 12:1–4.)

2. How did God thwart Herod Agrippa's plan? (See Acts 12:5–10, 18–19.)

3. How would you describe Herod Agrippa's relationship to God? What was the result of his attitude? (See Acts 12:21–24.)

4. What had Herod the Great done that no doubt influenced his grandson? (See Matthew 2:13–16.)

5. What does this example of Herod emphasize concerning the legacy each of us will leave and the way in which the values of parents and grandparents can influence their children?

DATA FILE

The Legacy of the Herods: Generations of Hardened Hearts
The Herod family had many encounters with Jesus and His message, yet no one in this family believed.

Herod the Great	Learned about Jesus' birth from the wise men. Responded by trying to kill the infant Jesus (Matthew 2:1–16).
Antipas (Herod the Great's son)	Heard about Jesus; listened to John the Baptist's teachings; met Jesus but sent Him to Pilate (Mark 6:14–20; Luke 23:8–12).
Agrippa I (grandson of Herod the Great) to whom Emperor Claudius gave Herod the Great's entire kingdom.	Arrested Christians; had James put to death; imprisoned Peter; had to figure out how Peter escaped (Acts 12:1–5, 18–19). Died when he allowed people to treat him like a god (Acts 12:21–23).
Drusilla (daughter of Agrippa I)	Listened to Paul as he spoke about faith in Christ Jesus (Acts 24:24–26).
Agrippa II (great-grandson of Herod the Great)	Discussed Paul's case in Caesarea with governor Festus; heard Paul's conversion testimony; recognized that Paul was trying to persuade him to become a Christian (Acts 25:13–14, 23; 26:1–29).
Bernice (great-granddaughter of Herod the Great)	Accompanied Agrippa II and heard Paul's conversion testimony (Acts 25:13–14, 23; 26:1–29).

THE HEROD FAMILY TREE

Antipater (Idumaean)

HEROD THE GREAT

- Died in 4 B.C.
- Effective administrator, cruel, supported by Rome
- Visited by wise men, killed Bethlehem babies
- Greatest builder the ancient Near East ever knew
- Had 10 wives, three of whom were:

Cleopatra	Miriam	Malthace	

PHILIP

- Effective, popular king
- Ruled north and east of Galilee
- Built Caesarea Philippi

(Luke 3:1)

ANTIPAS

- Effective king
- Ruled Galilee and Perea
- Killed John the Baptist
- Built Tiberias and Sepphoris
- Tried Jesus before crucifixion

(Luke 3:19; Luke 23:7–12; Luke 9:7–9; Matthew 14:1–12 Luke 13:32)

ARCHELAUS

- Poor ruler, deposed by Romans
- Ruled Judea
- Mary and Joseph settle in Nazareth to avoid him

(Matthew 2:22)

HEROD AGRIPPA I

(Grandson of Herod the Great)

- King of Judea
- Killed James, put Peter in prison
- Struck down by an angel

(Acts 12:1–24)

AGRIPPA II

- King of Judea
- Paul defends his faith before him

(Acts 25:13–26:32)

DRUSILLA

(Sisters of Agrippa II)

- Married Felix, the Roman governor

(Acts 24:24)

BERNICE

- With her brother at Paul's defense

(Acts 25:13)

Topic C: Jesus' Testimony to a Culture Shaper

1. Who was Pilate? (See Matthew 27:11.)

2. What do the questions Pilate asked of Jesus in the following verses reveal about Pilate?

    Matthew 27:11

    Matthew 27:13

    Matthew 27:17

    Matthew 27:19–21

    John 18:36–38

3. What do Jesus' answers to Pilate (John 18:33–37) reveal about His desire to tailor His message to fit Pilate's pagan worldview?

4. To whom are Jesus' followers called to be witnesses? (See Matthew 28:19–20; Acts 1:8; Luke 21:10–13.)

Topic D: Caesarea—Launching Point for Spreading the News of Jesus

Herod built a seaport and cosmopolitan city that would play a vital role in spreading the news of Jesus throughout the Gentile world, even though Herod built them solely to bolster his ego and glorify himself.

1. Where did Philip share Jesus' message? (See Acts 8:40; 21:8.)

2. Where did the Gospel first reach the Gentiles? (See Acts 10:1, 24–33, 44–48.)

3. What role did Caesarea play in each of Paul's missionary journeys?

    Acts 9:30; 13–14

    Acts 15–18

    Acts 18–21

    Acts 27–28

4. Because of a plot against Paul's life, he was sent to which city where he was able to share Christ with two Roman governors and Herod Agrippa II? (See Acts 23:23–24, 27; 25:1–6, 23.)

DATA FILE

Herod Built the Seaport at Caesarea Because He:

- Needed a port on the Mediterranean because existing ones were outside his kingdom or hostile to him.
- Recognized Caesarea's strategic location along the Via Maris, the trade route between Rome and such regions as Persia, Babylonia, the Orient, and the Arabian Peninsula.
- Needed a vast source of revenue to fund his great building projects, such as the Temple Mount in Jerusalem, his palace at Masada, and Jericho.
- Sought to expand his influence, both to curry favor with Rome and to bring Roman culture and military support to Judea.
- Wanted to demonstrate his greatness.
- Needed to create a buffer zone to keep the Parfians and Idumeans out of the Roman Empire.

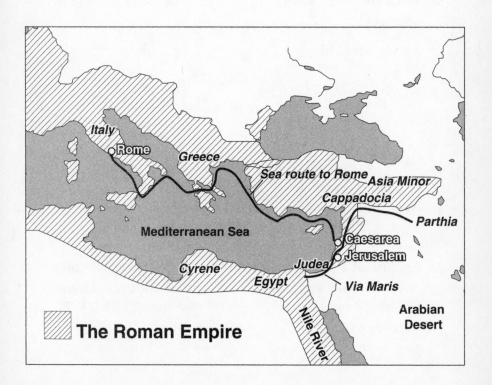

ᖴaith Lesson

Time for Reflection

Read the following passage of Scripture silently and consider how the apostle Paul used his time and energy while imprisoned in Caesarea to proclaim the truth of the gospel to the surrounding secular culture. Then reflect on how God might have you bring Jesus' message to your world.

> Then he called two of his centurions and ordered them, "Get ready a detachment of two hundred soldiers, seventy horsemen and two hundred spearmen to go to Caesarea at nine tonight. Provide mounts for Paul so that he may be taken safely to Governor Felix."

> ACTS 23:23–24

More than two years later:

> ... Agrippa and Bernice came with great pomp and entered the audience room with the high ranking officers and the leading men of the city. At the command of Festus, Paul was brought in.... Then Agrippa said to Paul, "You have permission to speak for yourself." So Paul motioned with his hand and began his defense: "King Agrippa, I consider myself fortunate to stand before you today as I make my defense against all the accusations of the Jews, and especially so because you are well acquainted with all the Jewish customs and controversies. Therefore, I beg you to listen to me patiently.... So then, King Agrippa, I was not disobedient to the vision from heaven. First to those in Damascus, then to those in Jerusalem and in all Judea, and to the Gentiles also, I preached that they should repent and turn to God and prove their repentance by their deeds. That is why the Jews seized me in the temple courts and tried to kill me. But I have had God's help to this very day, and so I stand here and testify to small and great alike. I am saying nothing beyond what the prophets and Moses said would happen—that the

Christ would suffer and, as the first to rise from the dead, would proclaim light to his own people and to the Gentiles." At this point Festus interrupted Paul's defense. "You are out of your mind, Paul!" he shouted. "Your great learning is driving you insane." "I am not insane, most excellent Festus," Paul replied. "What I am saying is true and reasonable. The king is familiar with these things, and I can speak freely to him. I am convinced that none of this has escaped his notice, because it was not done in a corner. King Agrippa, do you believe the prophets? I know you do." Then Agrippa said to Paul, "Do you think that in such a short time you can persuade me to be a Christian?" Paul replied, "Short time or long—I pray God that not only you but all who are listening to me today may become what I am, except for these chains."

ACTS 25:23; 26:1–3, 19–29

1. Paul, even though he was a prisoner, boldly presented Jesus' message to the Gentile authorities in Caesarea. Are you eager to testify of the truth of the gospel to non-Christians, or do you tend to "hide" from secular culture?

2. In Caesarea, as in our culture today, a war for the souls of people was being fought. Note the many ways in which Paul sought to convince his listeners of the truth of the gospel message. How might you bring Jesus' message to the people around you this week? In what ways can you present the gospel?

3. God gave Paul education, intelligence, eloquence, bold-
    ness—wonderful stones with which to build a legacy. Even
    when he was imprisoned and his sphere of influence was
    limited by others, he used every opportunity to deliver the
    message of Jesus the Messiah to the secular culture. What
    limits your sphere of influence? Given that limitation, what
    opportunities do you have to deliver the gospel message?

Action Points

Take a moment to review the key points you explored today. Then
write down an action step (or steps) that you will commit to this week
as a result of what you have discovered.

1. *Herod built magnificent buildings, a harbor, and a seaport
    in Caesarea, yet all that's left of Herod's legacy are broken
    pieces of marble and stone—broken pieces of his dreams.*
    He lived to promote himself, and his greatness is of no con-
    sequence today.

    In contrast, a boy named David used a common stone to
    kill Goliath and honor God. What David did to Goliath in
    the valley of Elah is a witness to what happens when a per-
    son uses his or her life to honor God and point other
    people toward Him. David lived in obedience to God ...
    and his memory lives on. In fact, Jesus was born into the
    lineage of David—and lives today as the "chosen and pre-
    cious cornerstone" of our faith (1 Peter 2:6).

    God has given each of us "stones" with which to build a
    legacy—talents, opportunities, resources, training, intel-
    ligence, networks. How are you using the life-building
    "stones" God has given you? For whom are you building?
    Are you building your life around yourself, in which case
    other people will someday pick up the broken pieces of

your dreams? Or are you building for God, honoring Him with your life and building something that will last for eternity?

2. *God used what Herod—a self-centered genius who rejected God and highly esteemed pagan values—built in Caesarea in order to spread the gospel.* First, God poured His Spirit upon influential Gentiles in that city with whom Peter had shared the gospel. Then Paul stood in the city that Herod had built and proclaimed the gospel to the highest rulers of that region. Paul and other early missionaries used Herod's seaport in their travels, which spread the gospel message to more distant lands.

   Just as God used Caesarea to promote His kingdom, He has used technological and man-made advances to help spread the gospel. Which resources available to you could be used to further the kingdom of God, to address the pagan values and practices in our own culture?

   How will you use your resources to honor God and draw other people closer to Him this week?

3. *Caesarea stood at the crossroads of culture, near the ancient trade route called the Via Maris.* There, the first Christians shared the message of Jesus with powerful people who shaped their culture. Those first Christians

were like standing stones. God placed them on the cross-roads of the world so that their lives could point people toward God. In that pagan city, the Christians spoke and acted boldly, even though they were sometimes ridiculed and persecuted. As a result, many people around the world—including modern-day non-Jewish Christians—came to know Israel's God and His Messiah.

Now it's your turn. You live at a crossroads. The world is watching you. You must make a choice. Will you succumb to the self-indulgent and self-glorifying culture of our day? Will you allow your culture to woo you away from God and encourage you to seek pleasure apart from God? Or will you act as a standing stone, boldly proclaiming God's message? Will you live out your commitment to Him to a watching world?

Where do you stand? What is your choice?

additional resources

History

Connolly, Peter. *Living in the Time of Jesus of Nazareth*. Tel Aviv: Steimatzky, 1983.
Ward, Kaari. *Jesus and His Times*. New York: Reader's Digest, 1987.
Whiston, William, trans. *The Works of Josephus: Complete and Unabridged*. Peabody, Mass.: Hendrikson Publishers, 1987.
Wood, Leon. Revised by David O'Brien. *A Survey of Israel's History*. Grand Rapids: Zondervan, 1986.

Jewish Roots of Christianity

Stern, David H. *Jewish New Testament Commentary*. Clarksville, Md.: Jewish New Testament Publications, 1992.
Wilson, Marvin R. *Our Father Abraham: Jewish Roots of the Christian Faith*. Grand Rapids: Eerdmans, 1986.
Young, Brad H. *Jesus the Jewish Theologian*. Peabody, Mass.: Hendrickson Publishers, 1995.

Geography

Beitzel, Barry J. *The Moody Atlas of Bible Lands*. Chicago: Moody Press, 1993.
Gardner, Joseph L. *Reader's Digest Atlas of the Bible*. New York: Reader's Digest, 1993.

General Background

Alexander, David, and Pat Alexander, eds. *Eerdmans' Handbook to the Bible*. Grand Rapids: Eerdmans, 1983.
Butler, Trent C., ed. *Holman Bible Dictionary*. Nashville: Holman Bible Publishers, 1991.
Edersheim, Alfred. *The Life and Times of Jesus the Messiah*. Peabody, Mass.: Hendrickson Publishers, 1994.

Archaeological Background

Charlesworth, James H. *Jesus Within Judaism: New Light from Exciting Archaeological Discoveries*. New York: Doubleday, 1988.
Finegan, Jack. *The Archaeology of the New Testament: The Life of Jesus and the Beginning of the Early Church*. Princeton: Princeton University Press, 1978.
Mazar, Amihai. *Archaeology of the Land of the Bible: 10,000–586 B.C.E.* New York: Doubleday, 1990.

To learn more about the specific backgrounds this set of videos, consult the following resources:

Avigad, Nahman. "Jerusalem in Flames—The Burnt House Captures a Moment in Time." *Biblical Archaeology Review* (November-December 1983).
Barkey, Gabriel. "The Garden Tomb—Was Jesus Buried Here?" *Biblical Archaeology Review* (March-April 1986).
Ben Dov, Meir. "Herod's Mighty Temple Mount." *Biblical Archaeology Review* (November-December 1986).
Bivin, David. "The Miraculous Catch." *Jerusalem Perspective* (March-April 1992).
Burrell, Barbara, Kathryn Gleason, and Ehud Netzer. "Uncovering Herod's Seaside Palace." *Biblical Archaeology Review* (May-June 1993).
Edersheim, Alfred. *The Temple*. London: James Clarke & Co., 1959.
Edwards, William D., Wesley J. Gabel, and Floyd E. Hosmer. "On the Physical Death of Jesus Christ." *Journal of American Medical Association (JAMA)* (March 21, 1986).
Flusser, David. "To Bury Caiaphas, Not to Praise Him." *Jerusalem Perspective* (July-October 1991).
Greenhut, Zvi. "Burial Cave of the Caiaphas Family." *Biblical Archaeology Review* (September-October 1992).
Hareuveni, Nogah. *Nature in Our Biblical Heritage*. Kiryat Ono, Israel: Neot Kedumim, Ltd., 1980.
Hepper, F. Nigel. *Baker Encyclopedia of Bible Plants: Flowers and Trees, Fruits and Vegetables, Ecology*. Ed. by J. Gordon Melton. Grand Rapids: Baker, 1993.
"The 'High Priest' of the Jewish Quarter." *Biblical Archaeology Review* (May-June 1992).
Hirschfeld, Yizhar, and Giora Solar. "Sumptuous Roman Baths Uncovered Near Sea of Galilee." *Biblical Archaeology Review* (November-December 1984).
Hohlfelder, Robert L. "Caesarea Maritima: Herod the Great's City on the Sea." *National Geographic* (February 1987).
Holum, Kenneth G. *King Herod's Dream: Caesarea on the Sea*. New York: W. W. Norton, 1988.
Mazar, Benjamin. "Excavations Near Temple Mount Reveal Splendors of Herodian Jerusalem." *Biblical Archaeology Review* (July-August 1980).
Nun, Mendel. *Ancient Stone Anchors and Net Sinkers from the Sea of Galilee*. Israel: Kibbutz Ein Gev, 1993. (Also available from *Jerusalem Perspective*.)
_____. "Fish, Storms, and a Boat." *Jerusalem Perspective* (March-April 1990).
_____. "The Kingdom of Heaven Is Like a Seine." *Jerusalem Perspective* (November-December 1989).
_____. "Net Upon the Waters: Fish and Fishermen in Jesus' Time." *Biblical Archaeology Review* (November-December 1993).
_____. *The Sea of Galilee and Its Fishermen in the New Testament*. Israel: Kibbutz Ein Gev, 1993. (Also available from *Jerusalem Perspective*.)

Pileggi, David. "A Life on the Kinneret." *Jerusalem Perspective* (November-December 1989).

Pixner, Bargil. *With Jesus Through Galilee According to the Fifth Gospel.* Rosh Pina, Israel: Corazin Publishing, 1992.

Pope, Marvin, H. "Hosanna: What It Really Means." *Bible Review* (April 1988).

Riech, Ronny. "Ossuary Inscriptions from the Caiaphas Tomb." *Jerusalem Perspective* (July-October 1991).

_____. "Six Stone Water Jars." *Jerusalem Perspective* (July-September 1995).

Ritmeyer, Kathleen. "A Pilgrim's Journey." *Biblical Archaeology Review* (November-December 1989).

Ritmeyer, Kathleen, and Leen Ritmeyer. "Reconstructing Herod's Temple Mount in Jerusalem." *Biblical Archaeology Review* (November-December 1989).

_____. "Reconstructing the Triple Gate." *Biblical Archaeology Review* (November-December 1989).

Ritmeyer, Leen. "The Ark of the Covenant: Where It Stood in Solomon's Temple." *Biblical Archaeology Review* (January-February 1996).

_____. "Quarrying and Transporting Stones for Herod's Temple Mount." *Biblical Archaeology Review* (November-December 1989).

Ritmeyer, Leen, and Kathleen Ritmeyer. "Akeldama: Potter's Field of High Priest's Tomb." *Biblical Archaeology Review* (November-December 1994).

Sarna, Nahum M. *The JPS Torah Commentary: Exodus.* New York: Jewish Publication Society, 1991.

"Sea of Galilee Museum Opens Its Doors." *Jerusalem Perspective* (July-September 1995).

Shanks, Hershel. "Excavating in the Shadow of the Temple Mount." *Biblical Archaeology Review* (November-December 1986).

"Shavuot." *Encyclopedia Judaica,* Volume 14. Jerusalem: Keter Publishing House, 1980.

Stern, David. *Jewish New Testament Commentary.* Clarksville, Md.: Jewish New Testament Publications, 1992.

Taylor, Joan E. "The Garden of Gethsemane." *Biblical Archaeology Review* (July-August 1995).

Tzaferis, Vassilios. "Crucifixion—The Archaeological Evidence." *Biblical Archaeology Review* (January-February 1985).

_____. "A Pilgrimage to the Site of the Swine Miracle." *Biblical Archaeology Review* (March-April 1989).

_____. "Susita." *Biblical Archaeology Review* (September-October 1990).

Vann, Lindley. "Herod's Harbor Construction Recovered Underwater." *Biblical Archaeology Review* (May-June 1983).

FAITH LESSONS VIDEO SERIES

Ray Vander Laan

Filmed on location in Israel, **Faith Lessons** is a unique video series that brings God's Word to life with astounding relevance. By weaving together the Bible's fascinating historical, cultural, religious, and geographical contexts, teacher and historian Ray Vander Laan reveals keen insights into Scripture's significance for modern believers.

> *"Nothing has opened and illuminated the Scriptures for me quite like the Faith Lessons series."* —Dr. James Dobson

Faith Lessons on the Promised Land, Crossroads of the World: Volume One 0-310-67864-1
Faith Lessons on the Prophets & Kings of Israel: Volume Two 0-310-67865-X
Faith Lessons on the Life & Ministry of the Messiah: Volume Three 0-310-67866-8
Faith Lessons on the Death & Resurrection of the Messiah: Volume Four 0-310-67867-6

JESUS

An Interactive Journey

Now, through the cutting-edge technology of interactive CD-ROM, you can make an incredible voyage—back to the life and times of Jesus! This exciting multimedia adventure takes you there, giving you an entirely new appreciation for the fascinating historical, geographical, and cultural backdrop that will enhance your understanding of the Gospel.

The high technology and vast amount of material in this unique presentation will captivate you for hours, while providing a solid understanding of the Gospel and its relevance to today's believer. It's great for personal and family Bible study, Christian schools, and a wide variety of church uses.

Compatible with Windows® 95 and Windows® 3.1

CD-ROM 0-310-67888-9

ECHOES OF HIS PRESENCE

Ray Vander Laan

Through historically accurate, fictional stories of people Jesus touched, *Echoes of His Presence* spans the gap between the history of Jewish tradition and the nature of Western thinking, making the Savior's ministry relevant, significant, and more meaninful than ever to today's believers. You'll undestand Scripture in its cultural context . . . and you'll fall in love with Jesus all over again.

Hardcover 0-310-67886-2
Audio 0-310-67887-0

Zondervan Publishing House
Grand Rapids, Michigan
http://www.zondervan.com

A Division of HarperCollinsPublishers